Releasing the Angel

Releasing the Angel

Saluting All Who Strive to Teach

Christopher Gleeson SJ

ATF Press
Adelaide

First published 2008

National Library of Australia
Cataloguing-in-Publication data
Gleeson, Christopher, 1943- .
       Releasing the angel : saluting all those who strive to
       teach.

       Includes index.
       ISBN 9781920691967 (pbk.).

       1. Teachers. 2. Christian teachers. 3. Church and
       education. 4. Teaching - Religious aspects - Christianity.
       I. Title.

371.1008827

Cover graphic by Simon Brushfield.
Cover design by Astrid Sengkey.

ATF Press
An imprint of the Australasian Theological Forum Ltd
PO Box 504
Hindmarsh
SA 5007
ABN 90 116 359 963
www.atfpress.com

Contents

Dedication

I dedicate this book to all those life enlargers who have taught me and taught with me over the years. Thank you for your inspiration in teaching yourselves.

Just recently I was leafing through my office bookcase at Banyo and came across an early edition of my book *Striking a Balance: Teaching Values and Freedom*. Inside the cover I had written at the book launch:

'Dear Mum,

Thank you for being my first and best teacher of values.

Much love,

Chris

25 June 1993'

Acknowledgements

Several friends and colleagues have taken the time to read these words and offer constructive suggestions for their improvement. Brother Bill Firman FSC, with characteristic generosity and meticulous care, offered me very helpful advice about the whole text and its layout. I am most appreciative too for the time that Dr Leoni Degenhardt gave to reading the text and writing a generous tribute for the cover. Joe McCorley's enthusiasm was a strong motivating force for me to awaken from my unworthy lethargy and extract the book from the computer for publication by a very energetic and efficient publisher. Bob Grant and Bebe McEncroe were also supportive in getting the book across the line, while Trish O'Brien's creative flair prompted various decisions about the use of colour and graphics. Several teachers offered me various quotations that have inspired them on their journey and I have used them gratefully. Clearly, any deficiencies and limitations in the final product can be attributed to the author.

I am delighted and grateful that family friend and former student, Simon Brushfield, has allowed me to use his beautiful art work to illustrate the cover and middle section of the book. His deft use of colour and symbol both enhance the text and challenge the reader to find deeper meanings in it.

As with other books I have written, the extracts, quotations and poetry in this latest collection have been brought together over many years and from various periods of my life. Every effort has been made to trace the origins for all the material in this book, but some sources remain missing in action. I am grateful to those authors, both known and unknown, named or unnamed, whose material I have valued and quoted in this publication.

Foreword

Ancient wisdom says that all of us, at any given time, might be 'entertaining angels unawares'. Angels lurk everywhere in education. Indeed, it is written in the Talmud that 'every blade of grass has its Angel that bends over it and whispers, "grow, grow"'.

In the March 2005 edition of western Sydney's Loyola Senior High School newsletter, Jesuit Principal Brendan Kelly wrote movingly: 'When is the last time you were surprised by an angel? They visit us all the time, angels. The world is full of God's messengers. You know them. They are the people and events who come out of nowhere, cross our path and point us in a direction that we hadn't thought of, or say that word that makes the difference or leave us feeling amazed or full of wonder. Wonderful beings, angels! I encountered one recently. I received a telephone call from a former student. She asked me to contact her girlfriend who works at Parramatta Gaol. I dutifully telephoned. 'Can you come and visit a young man who has been in custody for two months? He wants an Easter blessing.'

Schools abound in Angels and not all of them are women or teachers! The school doctor, the head cleaner, the nurse, the canteen director, the front desk receptionist, the Principal's secretary—are just a few of those people in our school communities whose angelic quality connects us to God.

The story is told of the man visiting Michelangelo in his studio as he was chipping away with his chisel at a huge shapeless block of marble. He was surrounded by dust and covered in fragments. It was not a pretty sight. The man asked Michelangelo what he was doing, and he replied: 'I'm releasing the angel imprisoned in this marble.'

Education, as the word implies, is that profession which seeks to free people—to give each individual the care, the wherewithal, to achieve their potential. Often we ourselves are blind to these gifts and talents and they can only be released for us, even chiseled out of us, by teachers who have a vision and a love to set them free. Clearly, the teacher has enormous power and responsibility in his or her hands. The good teacher is an enabler, one who enables and empowers their pupils to take on wings. The teacher is he or she who frees, who liberates from ignorance and thus releases the child for the energies of the mind and the imagination, without which no-one would ever be fully alive or fully human. As with the priesthood, the aim of teachers is 'to give wings to the soul' (St Gregory Nazianzen).

It would take very little for us, I am sure, to recall teachers and colleagues who have been true educators, true liberators for us in this sense. This little book of reflections is both a tribute to these people and, hopefully, a source of inspiration for all who are committed to the vocation of teaching.

And it is, indeed, a vocation. Jonathan Sacks, the inspirational Chief Rabbi of the Commonwealth, wrote in 2001:

> To want the best for our children is to want the best teachers for our children. They are the guardians of our culture, the trustees of our future. Teachers need to be paid enough to live without financial worry, to attract the brightest and best to the profession and to signal to every child in every classroom that this teacher is a role model and this career a vocation to which it is honourable to aspire. Civilisations that honour teachers survive and flourish. Civilisations that don't, just don't. That is our choice. And friends, that is the history lesson that all of us must go back to the classroom to learn.

Wenona Principal, Margaret Hadley, echoed these sentiments in December, 2004, when she wrote in her Principal's Report: 'I would go so far as to claim that teachers are the most under valued resource in our present society. How often do we hear parents demanding the "best" teachers for their children, but would never want their own child to become a teacher. Teachers are not a renewable resource . . .'

Authors Thomas Landy (Thomas Landy, 'Collegium and the Intellectual's Vocation to Serve', 21) and Margaret Wheatley (Margaret J Wheatley, 'Leadership in Turbulent times is Spiritual', 2002) make a similar point about the nobility of the teaching vocation. For Landy 'vocation is that sense that nourishes us in our best moments. We sense that we are for some reason meant to do what we are doing, that our work is of inherent value to others and to us, not merely a way of passing the days or collecting a cheque. The origin of that sense of purpose lies outside of ourselves—it is not merely an invention of our own selves—yet is intimately connected to who we are as individuals, to our own particular gifts, talents, and sources of contentment . . .'

Margaret Wheatley writes:

> We don't decide what our vocation is, we receive it. It always originates from outside us. Therefore, we can't talk about vocation or calling without acknowledging that there is something going on beyond our narrow sense of self. It helps remind us that there's more than just me, that we're part of a larger and purpose-filled place . . . The stronger our sense of vocation, the more resilient and courageous we are. And we can only develop a sense of purpose or vocation from believing in a power and order greater than our own.

Former American Secretary of State Dag Hammersjkold puts it even more succinctly. 'For someone whose job so obviously mirrors man's extraordinary possibilities and responsibilities, there is no excuse if he loses his sense of "having been called". So long as he keeps that, everything he can do has a meaning,

nothing a price. Therefore: if he complains, he is accusing—
himself.'

Dag Hammarskjold, *Markings*, (23.6.57)

The framework for this book is very simple. Apart from this
Foreword and an explanatory note and Epilogue, the various
reflections are divided into six categories or chapters, each
with a Preview Window, that portrays the actions of Jesus the
Teacher as he accompanies those two slow learners on the road
to Emmaus in the Gospel of Luke. First of all, Jesus walks with
these two disciples who are distraught and disillusioned after the
events of Good Friday. He is, in the first instance, therefore, *a
companion*. His next challenge is to hear them out, *to listen carefully*
to their story of disappointment and disorientation. From being
the listener, Jesus becomes *the storyteller*, painting a big picture of
salvation history to help the two disciples understand the events
of Good Friday and Easter Sunday and place them in proper
perspective. Having told his story, Jesus motions to move on,
not wishing to impose himself on his two companions. It is Jesus
the liberator, the healer, the one who leaves his students free. The
three of them sit down for a meal together, and Jesus breaks the
bread and blesses it. Immediately, the two disciples recognise
Him. *Blessing* always brings illumination because it places
everything in proper context. To bless someone or something
is to acknowledge their true place in life as coming from God
and ending in Him. Jesus finally parts company with his two
companions, sending them back to encourage their colleagues
huddled together in fear and anxiety in the upper room. Good
teaching is ultimately about *community building.*

Questions About Angels

'Of all the questions you might want to ask
about angels, the only one you ever hear
is how many can dance on the head of a pin.

No curiosity about how they pass the eternal time
besides circling the Throne chanting in Latin
or delivering a crust of bread to a hermit on earth
or guiding a boy and girl across a rickety wooden bridge.

Do they fly through God's body and come out singing?
Do they swing like children from the hinges
of the spirit world saying their names backwards and
forwards?
Do they sit alone in little gardens changing colours?

What about their sleeping habits, the fabric of their robes,
their diet of unfiltered divine light?
What goes on inside their luminous heads? Is there a wall
these tall presences can look over and see hell?

If an angel fell off a cloud, would he leave a hole
in a river and would the hole float along endlessly
filled with the silent letters of every angelic word?

If an angel delivered the mail, would he arrive
in a blinding rush of wings or would he just assume
the appearance of the regular mailman and
whistle up the driveway reading the postcards?

No, the medieval theologians control the court.
The only question you ever hear is about
the little dance floor on the head of a pin
where halos are meant to converge and drift invisibly.

It is designed to make us think in millions,
billions, to make us run out of numbers and collapse
into infinity, but perhaps the answer is simply one:

one female angel dancing alone in her stocking feet,
a small jazz combo working in the background.

She sways like a branch in the wind, her beautiful
eyes closed, and the tall thin bassist leans over
to glance at his watch because she has been dancing
forever, and now it is very late, even for musicians.'

Billy Collins, *Sailing Alone Around the Room: New
and Selected Poems* (New York: Random House
Paperback, 2002), 24, 25

Some Pre-dispositions

'The readiness is all.'
Shakespeare

♦ 'Do not forget hospitality since in being hospitable some have
unknowingly entertained angels.'
Hebrews 13:2.

♦ 'I sometimes listen to something on radio 4 called "Thought
for the Day", remember "Thought for the Day". About 5
years ago the BBC cut down thought for the day from 3
minutes to 2 minutes and 45 seconds on the grounds that
nobody can concentrate for 3 minutes. So how is a teacher
going to deal with often unruly and violent children without
the support of the parents, the local community, the national
culture? It is impossible . . .'

Jonathan Sacks, 'Transforming Teacher Status. The
Future of the Teaching Profession 11th September
2001'

♦ 'It was Peter Berger, the American sociologist, who put it best when he spoke of the sense of humour as one of the "signals of transcendence" that break through into the human situation and remind us of something beyond . . . What we laugh at, we can rise above. Perhaps that is why Jews, along with other groups who have suffered much and suffered long, have developed a sense of humour as their defence against despair. Humour has something to do with hope.'

Chief Rabbi Jonathan Sacks, *The Times*, July 1998

♦ 'A hundred years from now it will not matter what my bank account was, the sort of house I lived in, or the kind of car I drove . . . but the world may be different because I was important in the life of a child.'

Poster

♦ 'Although I have not been able to check it out, two different scripture scholars have told me that Jesus is asked 183 questions directly or indirectly among the four gospels. Do you know how many of these he directly answers? Three! Jesus' idea of church is not about giving people answers but, in fact, leading them into liminal and dark space, where they will long and yearn for God, for wisdom and for their own souls.'

Richard Rohr, 'Liminal Space'

◆ 'From the place where we are right
     Flowers will never grow in the Spring.
     The place where we are right
     Is hard and trampled like a yard.
     But doubts and loves dig up the world
     Like a mole, a plough.'

                    Yehuda Amichai

◆ Parker Palmer in his book, *The Courage to Teach*, reminds us
  that 'good teachers possess a capacity for connectedness.
  They are able to weave a complex web of connections among
  themselves, their subjects, and their students so that students
  can learn to weave a world for themselves.' What will this
  look like in practice? The first thing to say is that teachers will
  not provide spiritual connectedness for their students unless
  they are connected people in their own inner worlds. There
  is a reluctance to use the word 'spiritual' or 'spirituality'
  stemming no doubt from its connotation with religion. Yet
  this is to restrict the proper meaning of a good word. The
  American author, Ronald Rolheiser, articulates this clearly
  for us when he says: 'Long before we do anything explicitly
  religious at all, we have to do something about the fire that
  burns within us. What we do with the fire, how we channel it,
  is our spirituality. Thus we all have a spirituality, whether we
  want one or not, whether we are religious or not. Spirituality
  is more about whether or not we can sleep at night than
  about whether or not we go to Church. It is about being
  integrated or falling apart, about being within community or
  being lonely, about being in harmony with mother earth or
  being alienated from her . . . What shapes our actions is our
  spirituality.' (Ronald Rolheiser, *Seeking Spirituality: Guidelines for
  a Christian Spirituality for the 21st Century*, Hodder & Stoughton,
  London, 1998), 6–7.

C Gleeson SJ, '"However Apart we are Together":
Addressing the Need for Connectedness in our
Young People'. *The Dorothy Knox Lecture,* 2002.
Teachers' Guild of New South Wales Annual
Conference

♦ In early June last year, while driving home from a meeting in the City, I tuned in to the late afternoon 'Drive' program on the ABC. The two guests on the program, Michael Rennie and Petria King, were telling listeners how to get in touch with the spiritual in their lives. Both had struggled with cancer and their fascinating advice came from lessons learnt in this struggle. Quoting Professor Ron Heifetz of Harvard University, Michael Rennie provided an excellent image for ourselves as teachers. He spoke about the balcony and the dance. In order to keep perspective on all the events going on around us every day, particularly in the frenetic pace of school life—the dance of life—we need to be able to get to the balcony to see all the patterns of movement on the dance floor. If we do not, we can easily be swept away by events. In his book, *Leadership Without Easy Answers*, Professor Heifetz gives the example of the Vietnam War when Lyndon Johnson 'got caught up in the unfamiliar dance of foreign policy and never got to the balcony. Besieged by expectations —his own, Washington's, and the American public's —Johnson engaged in the nation's conflict without ever leading it.'[1]

Teachers who are going to offer something to the inner world of students need to have a balcony in their life where they find connection and re-connection. What is that balcony for you? Is it a space, a time, a person?

C Gleeson SJ, *Dorothy Knox Lecture,* 2002

---

1. Ronald A Heifetz, *Leadership Without Easy Answers* (Cambridge MA: Belknap Press of Harvard University, 1994), 253.

An Explanatory Note

Those readers who were persistent enough to delve into *A Canopy of Stars: Some Reflections for the Journey* will know that I am an inveterate and unashamed 'scavenger' of others' thoughts and sayings. Rarely a day goes by that I do not commit to paper or memory some wise and inspiring words of people I meet along the way.

In *Releasing the Angel* I succumb to this addiction again. For the sake of clarity, I have written a short Preview Window prior to each chapter to shed some light on the sprinkling of quotations from various sources that follow. On each page there is a 'signpost' which seeks to focus a theme for those reflections. There are references from the Bible (using the New Jerusalem text), from books and articles, even some of my own written and spoken words over the years. Sometimes I offer a brief commentary on a topic and these are not in quotation marks. There is no real pattern in the sequence of quotations chosen, as I expect this is the sort of book people will read intermittently and to which they will return sporadically as the spirit moves them.

The symbols **A** and **Ω** on each page are the ancient Greek letters for Alpha and Omega, which are taken up in the Book of Revelation to describe the Lord Jesus as the Beginning and the End, 'the Lord God who is, who was, and who is to come, the Almighty' (Revelation 1:8).

'To see Thee is the end and the beginning,
Thou carriest us, and Thou dost go before,
Thou art the journey and the journey's end.'

Boethius

Clearly the inspiration for this book is Jesus the consummate Teacher, but I am hopeful that people of all religious persuasions, even those without any religious commitment, will find some value in the following pages.

All teachers are springtime workers in trusting that the seeds they sow in their students will produce one day people who make a difference in the wider community. *Releasing the Angel* issues from a similar act of faith that it will prove to be a book that teachers and others might leave open on their tables and from which they might glean some occasional inspiration.

Teaching and Accompanying

A WINDOW ON TEACHING AND ACCOMPANYING

These reflections focus on the quality of the relationship between Teacher and Student—getting to know and working with him or her, while always maintaining a professional balance between familiarity and distance.

In Luke 6:39 we hear Jesus saying: 'Can one blind person guide another? Surely both will fall into a pit?'

'Before the era of radio and television, a small-town telephone operator used to get a daily call requesting the exact time. She always gave it with confidence, because she set her watch daily when the town's only factory sounded its whistle. One day her watch stopped. When the daily call came, she explained that she was waiting for the factory whistle. She told the caller that she used it to set her watch each day. There was a silence. Then the caller said,

"This is the factory. We call you each day for the exact time to sound our whistle."

From Mark Link SJ, *Vision 2000 Cycle A* (Texas: Tabor Publishing, 1992), 327.

Signpost—TEACHING FOR ETERNITY

A

The Finest Profession

'For fifty years I was a teacher of literary scholarship and philosophical hermeneutics. Outstanding thinkers and poets write the letters. The teacher, the interpreter, is the postman, the *postino*, who does his best to put these letters in the right boxes. A humble profession. The great poet Hölderlin does not need Mr Steiner, but Mr Steiner passionately needs Hölderlin in order to be able to breathe in the realm of consciousness. These two activities should never be confused as too many of my university colleagues confuse them. I can tell you that many people take themselves very seriously in those surroundings. A humble profession but perhaps the finest that exists. What does it mean to be a teacher? Dante's answer is incomparable: m'insegnavate come l'uom s'eterna. Untranslatable: "Thou, my teacher, thou hast imparted to me how a human being turneth towards eternity, and maketh himself everlasting." How? Through study and commenting on texts, through the inexhaustible joys of learning by heart. (What one loves one learns by heart).'

George Steiner

'Each of us must make our own unique inner journey. Your journey will be different from mine, but we belong to one another, whether we are aware of it or not. I do not want anyone to follow my route, but I hope this book offers hope and direction to other staggering pilgrims and helps them to find their own direction. The signpost to follow is appreciation of our own worth . . . On the inner journey we find our own signpost, which points beyond ourselves and beyond our false values. The heart recognises the signpost; it reads: "You are precious in my eyes. You are honoured and I love you" (Isaiah 43:4).'

Gerard W Hughes, *Walk to Jerusalem: In Search of Peace*
(London: DLT, 1991)

Signpost—BREAKING BREAD

A

The word 'companion' comes from two Latin words—*cum* meaning 'with' and *panis* meaning 'bread'. A companion in the fullest sense of the word is one who breaks bread, shares a meal, with another. Sharing a meal with another can be such an intimate event. To share food with a person is to share life with them. Joan Chittister, quoting Judith Martin, writes: 'The dinner table is the centre for the teaching and practicing not just of table manners but of conversation, consideration, tolerance, family feeling, and just about all the other accomplishments of polite society except the minuet'.

Joan Chittister OSB, *Listen With the Heart: Sacred Moments in Everyday Life* (London: Sheed and Ward, 2001), 98, 99

Ω

'As soon as they came ashore they saw that there was some bread there, and a charcoal fire with fish cooking on it. Jesus said, "Bring some of the fish you have just caught".'

John 21:9–10

Signpost—THE TWO JOURNEYS IN LIFE

A

'But Ruth said, "Do not press me to leave you and to turn back
from your company, for

wherever you go, I will go,
wherever you live, I will live.
Your people shall be my people,
And your God, my God.
Wherever you die, I will die
And there will I be buried".'

Ruth 1:16–17

Ω

'As you move beyond school into the space where you will spend
the rest of your life, remember those two things. Firstly, journey
outwards, beyond what you now know, deliberately grow,
cultivate the skills of being a citizen of the wider world and live
in that wider space confidently.

Secondly, for God's sake, learn how to journey inwards,
into stillness; earnestly search out how to be in harmony with
the depth of being. Deliberately cultivate daily the habit of
silence.'

Professor Hedley Beare's advice about the two journeys in life
to the Upper School Speech Night at St Leonard's College,
Brighton, Victoria, on 9 December 1982

Signpost—TO TEACH WITH *AUTHORITY* IS TO NURTURE, CULTIVATE, AND GROW LIFE (from the Latin word *augere*—to add)

A

'Jesus had now finished what he wanted to say, and his teaching made a deep impression on the people because he taught them with authority, and not like their own scribes.'

Matthew 7:28–29

Ω

'I am a teacher.
I am a gateway to the universe.
I empower our youth.
I am an explorer, an experimenter, and an inventor.
I am proud of my ability.
I know what my students can do.
I am a leader, a trainer and a coach.
I am an achiever. I see new worlds evolving.
I know what my students need to succeed—and I believe they can.
I create the future every day.'

Jenny Lewis, in her Ann D Clark Lecture, 2004, quoted in Diocese of Parramatta *Our Catholic Schools*, Term 4, 2004

Signpost—TEACHING MUST BE LIFE GIVING

A

'I set before you life or death, blessing or curse. Choose life, then, so that you and your descendants may live, in the love of Yahweh your God . . .'

Deuteronomy 30:19

Ω

'As long as we can love each other, and remember the feeling of love we had, we can die without ever really going away. All the love you created is still there. All the memories are still there. You live on—in the hearts of everyone you have touched and nurtured while you were here.

His voice was raspy, which usually meant he needed to stop for a while. I placed the plant back on the ledge and went to shut off the tape recorder. This is the last sentence Morrie got out before I did: 'Death ends a life, not a relationship'.

Mitch Albom, *Tuesdays With Morrie* (Sydney: Hodder Headline, 1998), 174

Signpost—'EXAMPLE IS THE SCHOOL OF MANKIND'
Edmund Burke

'Today students do not listen seriously to teachers but to witnesses; and if they do listen to teachers, it is because they are witnesses.'

Pope Paul VI

'The philosopher Chuang Tzu says, "how shall I talk of the sea to a frog that has never left its pond?" How can we expect of them what we fail to be ourselves? What you are, you see, your students will be. What you have the courage to question, they will learn to question too.'

Joan Chittister OSB, 'Leading the Way: To go Where There is no Road—And Leave a Path', in Closing Address at the NCEA, USA, *National Catholic Reporter*, posted April 26, 2001

Signpost—GOOD TEACHING OFFERS PERSPECTIVE

A

'Teachers open our eyes to the world. They give us curiosity and confidence. They teach us to ask questions. They connect us to our past and future. They're the guardians of our social heritage. We have lots of heroes today—sportsmen, super-models, media personalities. They come, they have their fifteen minutes of fame, and they go. But the influence of good teachers stays with us. They are the people who really shape our life.'

Rabbi Jonathan Sacks, Chief Rabbi of the Commonwealth, 'Thought for the Day', 21 June 1999

Ω

'Saints do not see things others do not see. On the contrary. They see just what everyone else sees—but they see it differently.'

The 19th century American philosopher, Jonathan Edwards, quoted by that wonderful educator, Deirdre Rofe IBVM, in her 1998 Jesuit Lenten Series lecture on 'Education and Social Conscience'

Signpost—TEACHING AND PASSION

A

'Being a great teacher is a matter first and foremost of sensibility. One that unites passion, nobility and intellect, dignity and, above all, respect not only for students as they are but for what they can become.'

Helen Pringle, *The Australian,* 25 September 2002

Ω

'One student I heard about said she could not describe her good teachers because they were so different from each other. But she could describe her bad teachers because they were all the same: "Their words float somewhere in front of their faces, like the balloon speech in cartoons." With one remarkable image she said it all. Bad teachers distance themselves from the subject they are teaching and, in the process, from their students.'

Parker Palmer, 'The Heart of a Teacher', in *Change Magazine,* volume 29, number 6, November–December 1997

'So light for me has particular meaning, which is the light of the stars, which is why I'm drawn to astronomy, again. And I think also that you find God where your passion is, and my passion is the stars, so that's where I find God.'

Munya Andrews on Radio National 'The Spirit of Things', 13 March 2005

Signpost—LEARNING TO SEE WHAT IS IMPORTANT

A

'The real voyage of discovery lies not in seeking new landscapes but in having new eyes.'

Marcel Proust

Ω

'There is the story of the old Brazilian woman who crossed the Frontier border every day on a motor scooter with a sack of sand behind her. The customs officer eventually became suspicious and inquired: "Madam, what have you got in that sack?" "Only sand, sir", she replied. The officer emptied the sack and, indeed, it contained nothing but sand. And so it went on for a month. One day, becoming very frustrated, the officer said to the old woman, "I won't arrest you or say anything to the police, but just tell me: are you smuggling or not?" "Yes", she answered truthfully. "Well, what are you smuggling?" he pressed her. With a smile the old woman replied, "Motor Scooters".

Life is full of surprises and reality is not always what it appears to be on the outside. The great Christian writer, CS Lewis, said once: "When we get to Heaven, there will be three surprises. First, we will be surprised by the people that we find there, many of whom we surely had not expected to see. The second surprise is that we will be surprised by the people who are absent—the ones we did expect to see but who are not there. The third surprise, of course will be that *we're* there."

Jesus often explains in the Gospel what it is that makes some people real winners and others who lose the plot of life. It has nothing to do with anything outside us—nothing to do with money, reputation, power, status, or influence. It has everything to do with something inside us that makes us life's winners. It is a habit of the heart—of seeing who really needs us and then answering their call.'

C Gleeson SJ, Homily to Southwell House Mass, St Ignatius' College, 16 August 2001

Signpost—HUMANITY AND THE HEART

A

'Dear Teacher,

I am the victim of a concentration camp. My eyes saw what no man should witness: gas chambers built by learned engineers; children poisoned by educated physicians; infants killed by trained nurses; women and babies shot and burned by high school and college graduates. So I am suspicious of education. My request is help your students become human. Your efforts must never produce learned monsters, skilled psychopaths, educated Eichmanns.

Reading, writing and arithmetic are important only if they serve to make our children more human.'

From a Letter written by a Boston High School Principal to her new teaching staff each year (*The Tablet*, 10 October 1992)

Ω

'For where your treasure is, there will your heart be also.'

Luke 6:21

'Yet here was Morrie talking with the wonder of our college
years, as if I'd simply been on a long vacation.
"Have you found someone to share your heart with?" he asked.
"Are you giving to your community?"
"Are you at peace with yourself?"
"Are you trying to be as human as you can be?"'

Mitch Albom, *Tuesdays With Morrie* (Sydney: Hodder Headline,
1998), 34

Signpost—BUILDING RELATIONSHIPS

A

'Sometimes we pay too much attention to the content of teaching and not enough to the teacher-student relationship itself. It was Henri Nouwen who wrote that "the teaching relationship *is* the most important factor in the ministry of teaching".'

From Melannie Svoboda SND, *Teaching is like . . . Peeling back Eggshells* (Mystic,CT: Twenty-third Publicatons, 1995), 35

Ω

'Implicit in this whole emphasis is the idea that the relationship is more important than the content of one's communication . . .'

Michael Paul Gallagher SJ, *Struggles of Faith* (Dublin: The Columba Press, 1990), 64

'Teachers need enough time and flexibility to get to know kids as individuals. Teaching is about one and only one thing: getting to know the child. Getting inside his or her psyche. Getting close enough to learn something about his or her learning trajectory.'

Tom Peter, *Re-imagine! Business Excellence in a Disruptive Age* (London: Darling Kindersley, 2003), 284

Signpost—THE TEACHER'S ATTITUDE IS VITAL

A

'Christ has no body now but yours. No hands, no feet on earth but yours. Yours are the eyes through which he sees. Yours are the hands through which he does good.'

St Teresa

Ω

'I have come to a frightening conclusion. I am the decisive element in the classroom. It is my personal approach that creates the climate. It is my daily mood that makes the weather. As a teacher I possess tremendous power to make a child's life miserable or joyous. I can be a tool of torture or an instrument of inspiration. I can humiliate or humour, hurt or heal. In all situations it is my response that decides whether a crisis will be escalated or de-escalated, and a child humanised or de-humanised.'

From Haimg Ginott, *Teacher and Child* (New York, NY: Collie, 1972/1995), 15

'The longer I live I realise the impact of attitude on life. Attitude to me is more important than fact. It is more important than the past, than education, than money, than circumstances, than failures, than success, than what other people think or say or do. It is more important than appearance, giftedness, or skill. It will make or break a company, a church, and a home.

The remarkable thing is we have a choice every day regarding the attitude we will embrace for that day. We cannot change our past—we cannot change the fact that people will act in a certain way. We cannot change the inevitable. The only thing we can do is play on the one string we have, and that is our attitude.

I am convinced that life is 10% what happens to me and 90% how I react to it. And so it is with you.

You are in charge of your attitude.'

Charles Swindoll

Signpost—BEING EMPATHETIC AND HELPFUL

A

'It is important to note that students' perceptions of good teaching include both the instructional skills dimension and the empathy and caring dimension. They perceive both to be important in the learning partnership.'

From *Learner and Teacher : Perhaps the most Important Partnership of All,* Peter Westwood, Flinders University of South Australia. The Des English Memorial Lecture. AASE National Conference, Adelaide 1994

Ω

From hundreds of comments about good teaching collected from the students some common strands emerged. In general the students described a good teacher in the following terms.

* The good teacher:
    * Helps you with your work
    * Explains well so you can understand
    * Is friendly and easy to get on with, fair, straightforward
    * Makes lessons interesting and enjoyable
    * Cares about you, is always ready to listen, understands you
    * Has a sense of humour
    * Controls the class well
    * Knows what he or she is talking about

Signpost—TEACHING AND PERSONAL INTERACTION

A

Arguably the most important verse in the Scriptures (New Testament):

'While he was still a long way off, his father saw him and was moved with pity. He ran to the boy, clasped him in his arms and kissed him tenderly.'

Luke 15:21

Ω

'Being a teacher involves an intensely personal encounter. A swimmer also doesn't get to be a good swimmer by watching videos of swimming. It is the personal quality of the interaction that is essential.

I'm not implying you have to be a charismatic film star to be a good teacher. In Aristophanes' *Clouds*, a young student turns up at the Thinkery, an academy run by Socrates. Socrates is presented as a fluff-brain with none of the outward characteristics of the successful Athenian man: he is ugly, he doesn't wash, he waddles, and he doesn't speak properly. But he is a great teacher: the way Socrates talks about justice, the questions he asks are simple, powerful ones that often stop his interlocutors in their tracks.'

Helen Pringle, 'Best Instructors Stretch the Mind', in *The Australian*, Higher Education segment, 25 September 2002, 25

Gilbert Highett laid down three criteria for the good teacher: you must love your subject, love your students, and be utterly determined that they shall learn.

Signpost—FORMING MINDS AND CHARACTER

A

'"You defend a country by armies. But you defend a civilisation by schools." In a time of social instability, children needed more than ever a sense of "rootedness in a living tradition. We need to teach our children to hear the sound of eternity in the midst of change".'

Chief Rabbi of the Commonwealth, Dr Jonathan Sacks
Quoted in *The Tablet*, 9 July 1994

Ω

'What is a greater work
than to direct the minds and form the character of the young?
I hold with certainty that no painter, no sculptor, nor any other
artist does such excellent work as the one who moulds the
mind of youth?'

St John Chrysostom

Signpost—BE WHAT YOU TEACH

A

'We must teach more by example than by word.'

Blessed Mary MacKillop, 1867

'Preach the word wherever you go, even use words if necessary.'

St Francis of Assisi

Ω

'If the times are bad, then let us be better; then the times will be better, for we are the times.'

St Augustine

Signpost—LEADING TO THE SPIRITUAL

A

'To educate is to guide students on an inner journey toward more truthful ways of seeing and being in the world.

'How can schools perform their mission without encouraging the guides (we teachers)

. . . to scout the inner terrain.'

Parker Palmer, *The Courage to Teach: Exploring the Inner Landscape of a Teacher's Life* (San Francisco: Jossey-Bass, 1998)

Ω

'To be spiritual means to know, and to live according to the knowledge, that there is more to life than meets the eye.'

Richard McBrien, *Catholicism* (Minneapolis: Winston Press, 1980), para 1057

'And he went back to the fox.
"Good-bye", he said.
"Good-bye", said the fox. "And now here is my secret, a very simple secret: It is only with the heart that one can see rightly; what is essential is invisible to the eye."
"What is essential is invisible to the eye", the little prince repeated, so that he would be sure to remember.'

Antoine De Saint-Exupery,
The Little Prince (London: Penguin Puffin, 1969), 84

Signpost—THE COMPANION AS PEDAGOGUE

The classicists on staff have often reminded me that the word 'pedagogy' derives from the Greek and refers to the watchful slave or guardian whose responsibility it was to lead (*agagos*) the young boy (*paides*) to school. In other words, pedagogy is about companionship, care, and protection—a sort of leadership from behind.

A

'I am a little pencil in the hand of a writing God who is sending a love letter to the world.'

Mother Teresa

Ω

'One looks back with appreciation to the brilliant teachers, but with gratitude to those who touched our human feelings. The curriculum is so much necessary raw material, but warmth is the vital element for the growing plant and for the soul of the child.'

Carl Jung

Signpost—THE VALUE OF ENCOURAGEMENT

A

'18 March 2005

Dear Chris,

I have been meaning to write for many weeks now. Having taken up my new role (as Principal of a Catholic School) I find myself reflecting on some wonderful words of advice you gave me back in 1997 during some dark days in Boarding.

When I hit a very low point you said to me, "Chris, remember Good Friday always comes before Easter Sunday and you have to keep your eyes on the resurrection".

As I was preparing my speech for the next College Assembly using your wise words as the theme, I thought I would return the "precious gem".

Thank you for this and the many other gifts you gave me along the way!

Best wishes,

Chris Hayes.'

Ω

'God loves Teachers
On the sixth day God created men and women.
On the seventh day, God rested—not so much to recuperate but rather to prepare Himself for the work He would do on the eighth day.

For it was on that day that God created the first Teacher. This teacher, though taken from among men and women had several significant modifications. In general, God made the teacher more durable than other men and women.

God made the teacher tough—but gentle too.

God poured a generous amount of patience into the teacher.

God gave the teacher a heart slightly bigger than the average human heart. God gave the teacher an abundant supply of hope.

When God finished creating the teacher, He stepped back and admired His work. And God saw that the teacher was good, very good. And God smiled, for when he looked at the teacher, He saw into the future. He knew that the future is in the hands of each teacher.

Author unknown.'

Quoted in the St Ignatius School, Toowong. Newsletter, 27 October 2005

Signpost—LOOKING TO THE POSITIVE

A

'Just recently, I was reading a reflection by one of our graduates who was working in a Camphill Movement Community in Ballytobin, Ireland. He wrote: "Live-in voluntary work is intensive and provides no financial reward. However, you can gain great inner satisfaction when, for example, a young cerebral palsied boy called Nicholas learns to nod his head as well as give a verbal 'yes' response to a question asked of him; or when Jimmy Walsh, a hyperactive and autistic lad, suddenly, after one year's teaching, learns to tie up his shoe-laces. It is a nice experience." He goes on to quote the founder of the Camphill Movement who truly believed that "we do not deal with the handicapped child; we deal with the child who is handicapped". These people can change our lives. We do not work for them; we work with them.'

C Gleeson SJ, School Assembly—10 November 1998

Ω

'A passionate longing to grow, to become, is what we need.
There can be no place for the anemic in spirit,
the sceptics, the pessimists, the sad of heart,
the weary, the immobilists.
Life is ceaseless discovery
Life is movement.'

Pierre Teilhard de Chardin SJ

'No pessimist ever discovered the secrets of the stars, or sailed to an uncharted land, or opened a new heaven to the human spirit.'

Helen Keller

Signpost—PROBLEMS ARE FOR SHARING

A

'In recent days we have had the opportunity to reflect on the tragedy of suicide, and we need to keep a few things very clearly in mind. One thing is certain—suicide is permanent, but problems are temporary. No problem is permanent, no problem is such that we cannot find a solution to it. Our College has one of the best networks of pastoral care available to any school, and no problem is so big that we cannot find a solution or some relief to it. We have House Masters, Tutors, teachers, coaches, counsellors available to help you at all times. There is only one obligation when you have a problem—that is, you must tell someone about it. If you cannot speak to someone at school, then you must tell someone outside school. Problems only escalate, magnify in our minds, when we do not share them with another person.'

C Gleeson SJ, School Assembly 1 April 1998

Ω

Cynicism and its first cousin negativism are usually a refuge for the faint-hearted. In this context I have enjoyed quoting often the story of a young boy and his grandfather leading a donkey down a road. Someone laughed at them for being stupid and not riding the donkey. So the grandfather rode the donkey until someone criticised him for making the boy walk. Then the boy rode the donkey until someone criticised him for lack of respect for elders. Finally both rode the donkey until someone criticised them for being cruel to animals.

Signpost—COMPANIONSHIP IS HELPING TO
CARRY ANOTHER'S BURDENS

A

'The story is told of a man named Sundar who became a convert to Christianity and decided to stay in India to be a missionary and bear witness to Jesus. One late afternoon he was travelling on foot high in the Himalaya Mountains with a Buddhist monk. It was bitter cold, and the night was coming on. The monk warned that they were in danger of freezing to death if they did not reach the monastery before darkness fell.

It so happened that as they crossed over a narrow path above a steep cliff, they heard a cry for help. Deep down in the ravine a man had fallen and lay wounded. His leg was broken and he couldn't walk. So the monk warned Sundar, "Do not stop. God has brought this man to his fate. He must work it out by himself. That is the tradition. Let us hurry on before we perish." But Sundar replied, "It is my tradition now that God has brought me here to help my brother. I cannot abandon him." So the Buddhist monk left him and set off through the snow, which had started to fall heavily.

So Sundar climbed down to where the wounded man was. Since the man had a broken leg, Sundar took a blanket from his knap-sack and made a sling out of it. He got the man into it and hoisted him onto his back, then began the painful and arduous climb up the path. After a long time, he finally reached the path which he could barely see, and after much perseverance and exertion, he saw the lights of the monastery.

Then he nearly stumbled and fell. Not from weakness; he stumbled over an object lying on the path. He bent down on one knee and brushed the snow from the body of the Buddhist monk who had frozen to death within sight of the monastery. And there, kneeling on one knee in the snow, he understood for the first time what Jesus meant by his words: "For those who want to save their life will lose it, and those who lose their life for my sake will save it."

Years later when Sundar had his own followers, they asked this question: "Master, what is life's most difficult task?" And Sundar replied: "To have no burden to carry".'

Ω

'Come to me, all you who labour and are overburdened, and I will give you rest. Shoulder my yoke and learn from me, for I am gentle and humble in heart, *and you will find rest for your souls.* Yes, my yoke is easy and my burden light.'

Matthew 11:28–30

Signpost—THE HEART IS WHERE OUR TREASURE IS

A

'Today's Gospel about the Kingdom of Heaven as a treasure in a field reminds me of a story which the great Retreat Director, Father Tony De Mello, was fond of telling. It tells of the monk who, in his travels, found a precious gem stone and kept it. One day he met a fellow traveler, and when the monk opened his bag to share his food with him, the traveler saw the gem and asked the monk to give it to him. The monk did so readily.

The traveler then went on his way, overjoyed with the unexpected gift of the precious stone that was enough to give him wealth and security for the rest of his life. However, a few days later, he came back in search of the monk, found him, gave him back the gem stone, and made a special request of him: "Now please give me something much more precious than this stone, valuable as it is. Give me that which enabled you to give it to me in the first place.'

'Last week we received at the College a splendid letter from one of the Mothers of the children at our last Ignatian Children's Holiday Camp. For the last 4 years in December we have a conducted a 4 day Holiday Camp here at the College for some 25 very needy children around Sydney. It involves many of our senior students as carers for these young people, some senior girls from the Loreto schools, our own teaching and nursing staff, and some parents. This is part of what this Mother wrote to us last week: "Our son Douglas has autism. Autism is a severe brain disorder, which affects a person's ability to communicate, learn and interact with other people. The last 11 years have been difficult, frightening and bizarre. Of course, we have had many wonderful times with Douglas as he teaches us the important things in life. Nothing however had prepared me for the outpouring of love, care, concern and fun that Douglas received over the 4 day camp".'

C Gleeson SJ, School Assembly—28 August 2002

Ω

'Then Jacob awoke from his sleep and said, "Truly, Yahweh is in this place and I did not know".'

Genesis 28:16

Signpost—PRAYER RE-CONNECTS US

A

A Prayer for the 21st Century by John Marsden

'May the road be free for the journey
May it lead where it promised it would,
May the stars that gave ancient bearings
    Be seen, still be understood.
May every aircraft fly safely,
    May every traveler be found,
May sailors in crossing the ocean
Not hear the cries of the drowned.

May gardens be wild, like jungles,
    May nature never be tamed.
May dangers create of us heroes,
    May fears always have names.
May the mountains stand to remind us
    Of what it means to be young,
May we be outlived by our daughters,
May we be outlived by our sons.

May the bombs rust away in the bunkers,
And the doomsday clock not be rewound.
May the solitary scientists, working,
Remember the holes in the ground.
May the knife remain in the holder,
    May the bullet stay in the gun,
May those who live in the shadows
    Be seen by those in the sun.'

Ω

'When Jesus received this news he withdrew by boat to a lonely place where they could be by themselves. But the crowds heard of this and, leaving the town, went after him on foot. So as he stepped ashore he saw a large crowd; and he took pity on them and healed their sick.'

Matthew 14:13–14

Signpost—A TOLERANT COMPANION IS ONE WHO SHOULDERS ANOTHER'S BURDENS

A

'But uttering the word and holding out the hand of tolerance is not just for public figures and governments. Nor is it concerned only with the feelings and well being of indigenous Australians, though it must of course start there. It is something for every Australian. And as far as I am concerned, we need two hands of tolerance, ten fingers, ten principles of tolerance. This is what I suggest they should say:

Ten Principles of Tolerance

1. I will honour all human beings regardless of colour, race, or religion.
2. I will defend my neighbour against prejudice or discrimination.
3. I will live in a spirit of tolerance, friendship, and understanding.
4. I will reject any philosophy of racism whoever proclaims it.
5. I will protest against every expression of prejudice.
6. I will refuse to heed those who seek to set group against group or religion against religion.
7. I will not be part of any organisation that stands for racism or prejudice.
8. I will identify with all who spread tolerance and reconciliation.
9. I will do more than live and let live: I will live and help live.

10. I will not be deflected from this purpose even by fear of intimidation or victimisation.'

Rabbi Raymond Apple, Senior Rabbi of the Great Synagogue in Sydney—from an Address at the 'Sea of Hands' event in March, 1998

Ω

'I was a stranger and you made me welcome.'

Matthew 25:35

Signpost—LOVE IS A VERB, NOT A NOUN

A

'Love ought to show itself in deeds over and above words.'

The Spiritual Exercises of St Ignatius Loyola para 231

Ω

'Just before we came back to school for Term 4 we heard of the terrible bombing in Bali and the tragic loss and maiming of life suffered in that incident. On Monday this week we learnt of the shooting of students in an Economics class at Monash University in Melbourne—and all of this just a few short weeks since we prayed here in School Assembly remembering the first anniversary of the September 11 horrors in New York last year.

It is very easy to get caught up in the sadness of all these events, but I want today to point to just one of the stories of goodness and heroism, which shine out in these incidents as a light in the darkness. This story comes from the Bali tragedy and was reported in the *Daily Telegraph* last Saturday. On the Saturday night Lynley Huguenin "was battling for survival after she and friend Kim McKerrow were hit by the terrorist bomb. Covered in blood and suffering severe burns the two girls made it to the Kuta Paradiso Hotel and into the arms of their saviours Sevegne Newton and her partner David Sharp. "We walked in the door and screamed out for help—'somebody help'," Lynley said.

Sevegne heard the screams. "I said to David there's someone in pain", Sevegne said yesterday. "We both threw our clothes on and once we jumped into the lift and got down, I could see Lynley's blood all over the floor."

"She was saying 'please help me, can someone help me.'"

"We went downstairs and then we saw the blood."

"We just followed the blood and that's when we found her."

"I said to Lynley 'it's alright' and she said 'don't leave me, please don't leave me.'"

And Sevegne never did.

While Kim was taken by her parents to a military hospital for treatment, Sevegne and David stayed with 22-year old Lynley for the next 18 hours.

"It was the night from hell", Sevegne said.

Throughout the night and the next day, David and Sevegne sat with Lynley, bathed her wounds and called her parents.

Sevegne spoke to Lynley's father Barry in Melbourne and made a promise.

"I said 'I absolutely promise you that she will be home. I promise you I won't leave her'."

In the hopelessly overwhelmed hospital, Sevegne and David cared for Lynley as well as two Perth boys who were hit by shrapnel, a 15 year-old from Sydney and a young man from South Africa.

In all there were 15 people under their care and they made sure everyone of them made it out of Bali.

On Sunday night, David and Sevegne heard the first of the Hercules aircraft was arriving at Denpasar.

They rushed Lynley to the airport and David carried her on to the plane. She was the first bomb victim on board.

"I said 'I'll see you in Australia' Sevegne said." Yesterday she kept that promise.

Lynley's Mum Gail yesterday paid tribute to the couple who saved her daughter's life.

"We just love you, thank you. You're family now", she said.

To me this is a wonderful story of goodness, unselfishness and fidelity – that two strangers could go looking and find this terribly wounded young girl, stay with her for some 18 hours in hospital, put her on the first plane to Australia, and then go to visit her a week later in the Prince Alfred Hospital in Melbourne.'

C Gleeson SJ, School Assembly—22 October 2002

Signpost—LEARNING FROM BEING A COMPANION

A

'Life's Journey.
For each of us life is a journey.
Birth is the beginning of the journey,
And death is not the end but the destination.
It is a journey that takes you from youth to age,
From innocence to awareness,
From foolishness to wisdom,
From weakness to strength and often back again,
From loneliness to friendship,
From pain to compassion
From fear to faith,
From defeat to victory and victory to defeat,
Until, looking backward or ahead,
We see that victory does not lie at some high point along the
way,
But in having made the journey, stage by stage.'

Adapted from an old Hebrew Prayer

Ω

'I am the resurrection. Anyone who believes in me, even
though that person dies, will live, and whoever lives and
believes in me will never die. Do you believe this?'

John 11:25–26

Signpost—ACCOMPANYING THOSE ON
THE MARGINS

A

'Last Sunday some 250,000 people walked across the Sydney Harbour Bridge in solidarity with our Aboriginal brothers and sisters in an effort to advance the national cause for Reconciliation. We had about 100 walkers from Riverview and I want to thank and congratulate them, although I would have hoped 1000 might have walked to promote such an important cause in our nation. As I said last time, our national community is divided and torn apart by these issues and we need to heal the rift and unite people. Sunday was a start, but only a start.

One of the most important aspects of being a welcomer and a visitor is that of standing in solidarity with those people who live on the margins of society. For Jesus these were people like tax collectors, lepers, and sex workers. This caused him to be misunderstood by many people, but this always happens when one takes risks and gets ones hands dirty. I am sure St Ignatius our Founder was misunderstood by many when he became involved with ministering to one of the most marginalised groups of people—the sex workers in 16th century Rome.

For ourselves, one of the most marginalised peoples in our society is our Aboriginal brothers and sisters. St Ignatius would have been proud of those Riverview people who walked last Sunday, though I am sure he would have wanted to ask me why there was not a 1000 from our school walking.'

C Gleeson SJ, School Assembly—31 May 2000

Ω

'You have already been told what is right and what Yahweh wants of you. Only this, to act justly, to love tenderly, and walk humbly with your God.'

Micah 6:8

Signpost—COMPANIONSHIP AND FIDELITY

A

'Learning is a treasure which follows its owner everywhere.'

An old Chinese Proverb

'This week one of the greats of the Riverview teaching staff retired after nearly 25 years of service. Recruited from St Augustine's, Brookvale, in 1977 by the Headmaster of the time, Father Peter Bernard Quin, Errol has been a shining light to all who have crossed his path over these years. A specialist teacher of English and History in Years 8, 9, and 10, he has been something of a forerunner to our Middle Schooling program initiated in recent times. The boys loved his classes because he had that deft, albeit rare, touch of a true scholar who could share his prodigious learning with his students. An old Chinese Proverb could have been written with Errol in mind: "Learning is a treasure which follows its owner everywhere.' At various times Errol has been Ricci Housemaster, where he enjoyed, rather ironically, sporting dominance that not even greats like Les Kirkpatrick could boast; Year 12 Form Prefect, College Archivist, where he could utilise his extensive professional and published expertise in this field; College Organist, where his music was a delight to many, particularly the Boarders who prevailed on him to remain playing for their Sunday Masses after he resigned from this position several years ago; and Editor of the annual "Our Alma Mater" which, recalling Mussolini's success in making the trains run on time, he produced without fuss or flurry every year in time for the boys to take home on Speech Day. Few people have done more than Errol Lea Scarlett to be faithful custodians of the school's memory. He told our rich story in his 1989 History of the College to which we can constantly return to verify the anecdotal in his careful and interestingly told research. The dust cover of that book mentioned that "his favourite aversions are exhibitionism, competition, and the exercise of power". We also know that his pet addictions are the love of learning and his personal faith in God. Typical of this genuinely gentle man, he wrote a note of thanks to me after our Jesuit Community Dinner for him this week: "In the wider world of Riverview I take many precious memories with me—colleagues and some of the finest boys one could hope to meet anywhere."

In saying *Au revoir* to Mr Lea Scarlett, we thank him for everything he has contributed to Riverview over 25 years and we hold him up as a shining light of the teaching profession— someone who St Ignatius would have called *insignis*.'

C Gleeson SJ, School Assembly—30 March2001

Ω

'Wisdom brings up her own children and cares for those who seek her. Whoever loves her loves life, those who seek her early will be filled with joy. Whoever possesses her will inherit honour, and wherever he walks the Lord will bless him.'

Wisdom 4:11–13

Signpost—ENCOURAGEMENT AND ENTHUSIASM

A

'When I think back on my own life, I know how much I owe to my teachers. There were my first teachers, my Parents John and Doreen Gleeson. There was Sister Bernadette PBVM, my Year 3 Teacher in Sacred Heart School, Sandringham, in Melbourne, who could not only manage 65 boys and girls in the one class, but was able to teach us brilliantly at the same time. There were History teachers like Jim Griffin at school and at Melbourne University, Professor Harold Bolitho; English teachers like Vincent Buckley and Peter Steele; in the Society of Jesus I have had some wonderful teachers in Fathers John Monahan, Pat O'Sullivan, Bill Dalton, John Scullion, and Tony Campbell. I have also taught with some outstanding teachers here at Riverview, at Xavier in Melbourne, and St Ignatius' High School in Cleveland in the United States.

In all these people there were at least two qualities – what we might call the 2 E's. Firstly, there was great ENTHUSIASM for their subject, and secondly there was the capacity to ENCOURAGE their students in every way possible.

In recognising all our teachers here today, let us remember the words of writer Pearl Buck:

> Only the brave should teach. The men and women whose integrity cannot be shaken, whose minds are enlightened enough to understand the high calling of the teacher, whose hearts are unshakeably loyal to the young, whatever the interests of those who are in power.
>
> There is no hope for our world unless we can educate a different kind of man and woman. I put the teacher higher than any other person today in world society, in responsibility and in opportunity. Only those who love

the young should teach. Teaching is not a way to make a livelihood; the livelihood is incidental. Teaching is a vocation. It is as sacred as priesthood, as innate as a desire, as inseparable as the genius which compels a great artist.

If a teacher has not the concern of humanity, the love for living creatures, the vision of the priest and of the artist, that person must not teach. Teachers who hate to teach can only have pupils who hate to learn. Great and true teachers think of the child, dream of the child, see visions not of themselves but in the flowering of the child into adulthood. They think of the child first and always not of themselves.

It takes courage to be a teacher and it takes unalterable love for the child; only the brave should teach.

There is a marvellous line in Robert Bolt's play, *A Man For All Seasons* when Thomas More asks Richard Rich, "Why not be a teacher—you'd be a fine teacher, perhaps a great one?" Rich replies, "And if I was, who would know it?" To which More responds, "You, your pupils, your friends, God—not a bad public that".'

C Gleeson SJ, School Assembly, celebrating World Teachers'
Day—9 November 2001

Ω

'Let the little children come to me; do not stop them; for it is to such as these that the Kingdom of God belongs.'

Mark 10:14

Signpost—THE TRUE VALUE OF TEACHING

A

What Teachers Make By Taylor Mali
(Or You can always go to law school if things don't work out)
'He says the problem with teachers is,
"What's a kid going to learn from someone who decided his
best
option in life was to become a teacher?"
He reminds the other dinner guests that it's true what they say
about teachers: Those who can, do; those who can't, teach.
I decide to bite my tongue instead of his and resist the
temptation to remind the dinner guests that it's also true
what they say about lawyers. Because we're eating,
after all, and this is polite company.
"I mean, you're a teacher, Taylor", he says.
"Be honest. What do you make?"
And I wish he hadn't done that (asked me to be honest)
because, you see, I have a policy about honesty and ass-kicking:
if you ask for it, I have to let you have it.
You want to know what I make?
I make kids work harder than they ever thought they could.
I can make a C+ feel like a Congressional medal of honor
and an A- feel like a slap in the face.
How dare you waste my time with anything less than
your very best.
I make kids sit through 40 minutes of study hall
in absolute silence.
No, you may not work in groups.
No, you may not ask a question.
Why won't I let you get a drink of water?
Because you're not thirsty, you're bored, that's why.
I make parents tremble in fear when I call home:

I hope I haven't called at a bad time,
I just wanted to talk to you about something Billy said today.
Billy said, "Leave the kid alone. I still cry sometimes, don't
you?"
And it was the noblest act of courage I have ever seen.
I make parents see their children for who they are and
what they can be.
You want to know what I make?
I make kids wonder,
I make them question.
I make them criticize.
I make them apologize and mean it.
I make them write.
I make them read, read, read.
I make them spell definitely beautiful, definitely beautiful,
definitely beautiful over and over and over again until they
will never misspell either one of those words again.
I make them show all their work in math.
And hide it on their final drafts in English.
I make them understand that if you got this (brains) then you
follow this (heart) and if someone ever tries to judge you
by what you make, you give them this (the finger).
Let me break it down for you, so you know what I say is true:
I make a goddamn difference! What about you?'

Ω

'To educate young people properly
We must love them all:
We must love them all equally.
To love young people
is to devote yourself completely to
teaching them
and to take all the means that a keen
imagination
can think of to form them in Gospel
values.'

St Marcellin Champagnat

Signpost—LOVING THOSE WE TEACH

A

Since Vatican II, it has become clear that we need a much more humble, more modest view of the Church—one that is inclusive, involving all the people of God in open listening and learning—Bishop, priests, lay people—rather than one part of the church being taught by another. We need a good deal more of what one writer has called 'walking the walk instead of only talking the talk. In brief, we need an ecclesiology of accompaniment, and our ministry to young people in Catholic schools offers us the most wonderful opportunities for this ministry of companionship.

Let me offer here a rather unusual, yet splendid example of this ministry of accompaniment. In 1637, that giant amongst those we later called the North American Jesuit martyrs, Jean De Brebeuf, wrote the following list of instructions for his Jesuit missionaries working with the Huron Indians:

You must love these Hurons, ransomed by the blood of the Son of God, as brothers; you must never keep the Indians waiting at the time of embarking; carry a tinder-box or a piece of burning-glass, or both to make fire for them during the day for smoking, and in the evening when it is necessary to camp, as these little services win their hearts; try to eat the food they offer you, and eat all you can, for you may not eat again for hours; eat as soon as the day breaks, for Indians, when on the road, eat only at the rising and setting of the sun; be prompt in embarking and disembarking and do not carry any water or sand into the canoe; be the least troublesome to the Indians; do not ask questions: silence is golden; bear with their imperfections, and you must try always to be and appear cheerful; share little gifts with them; always carry something during the portages; do not be ceremonious with the Indians; do not paddle unless you intend always to paddle; the Indians will keep later that opinion of you which they have formed during the trip; always show any other Indians you meet on the way a cheerful face and show that you readily accept the fatigues of the journey.

Ω

'Unless the Lord builds the house,
those who build it labour in vain.
Unless the Lord watches over the city,
the watchman stays awake in vain.'

Psalm 127

Signpost—THE QUALITY OF OUR COMPANIONSHIP

A

'To help our young people grow as "spiritual" people, possessing a strong quality of soul to cope with the future, we have to look carefully at the quality of our own companionship. Perhaps the most important ingredient in our companionship with others is our own self-awareness. We have to be so alert to what is going on in ourselves, so alive to our own agenda, so capable of listening to ourselves *before* we can be of any real assistance to others. We must become accustomed to tuning into our moods and the simple process of self-reflection this evokes. Out of what level is most of today being lived? Is it a whole host of surface and superficial things which is making me feel empty? Or is my day coming from a different source which brings me deep peace, the sort of consolation associated with the true self? Self-awareness, therefore, is vital to the quality of our companionship. If we are unable to hear what is going on in ourselves, we will so easily allow it to interfere with our listening to others.'

C Gleeson SJ, ACSSQ talk, 1994

Ω

'I turn 50 later this year but I'm not using that occasion to sit back and reflect on my life. reflection is a pursuit for the retired. I don't dwell on things.'

Lee Freedman, *Jetstar* Magazine, April–May 2006

Signpost—OUR COMPANIONSHIP NEVER ENDS

A

Prayer for the Journey

'O God, be for us

A companion in walking,

A guide at the crossroads,

A defence against dangers,

Shelter on the road,

Shade in the heat,

Light in the darkness,

Courage in dismay

And firmness in our uncertainty

So that, following you,

We may arrive safely at the end of the journey.'

Prayer said for the pilgrims on the Way of Santiago de
Compostela

Teaching and Listening

A WINDOW ON TEACHING AND LISTENING

These reflective pieces focus on the teacher as a communicator, on the power of his or her words, and the capacity for listening to oneself and one's God as essential preparation for effective listening to one's students.

Signpost—GOOD LISTENING IS HEALING FOR OTHERS

A

'Great healing is available when we listen to each other.'

Margaret Wheatley

Ω

'Oh, come to the water all you who are thirsty;
though you have no money come!
Buy corn without money, and eat,
And, at no cost, wine and milk.
Why spend money on what is not bread,
Your wages on what fails to satisfy?
Listen, listen to me, and you will have good things to eat
And rich food to enjoy.
Pay attention, come to me;
Listen, and your soul will live.'

Isaiah 55:1–3

Signpost—LISTENING FOR GOD IN THE HERE AND NOW

A

'God, scripture assures us, is not in the whirlwind. God is not in a plethora of anything—words, places, rituals, ecclesiastical games, or people. God is simply right where we are. Which, of course, is why God is so hard to find. We are always looking elsewhere.'

Joan Chittister OSB, *Called to Question: A Spiritual Memoir* (London: Sheed and Ward, 2004), 40

'God is not in the whirlwind, not in the blustering and show, Scripture teaches us. God is in the breeze, in the very atmosphere around us, in the little things that shape our lives. God is in the contradictions that assail us, in the circumstances that challenge us, in the attitudes that impel us, in the motives that drive us, in the life goals that demonstrate our real aspirations, in the burdens that wear us down, in the actions that give witness to the values in our hearts. God is in the stuff of life, not in the airy-fairy of fertile imaginations bent on the pursuit of the preternatural. God is where we are, including in the very weaknesses that vie for our souls.'

Joan Chittister OSB, in *How Can I Find God?,* edited by James Martin (Missouri: Triumph, 1997), 84–85

Ω

'Therefore, everyone who listens to these words of mine and acts on them will be like a sensible man who built his house on rock. Rain came down, floods rose, gales blew and hurled themselves against that house, and it did not fall: it was founded on rock.'

Matthew 7:24–25

Signpost—LISTENING AND LIFE-GIVING

A

'Listening is always a life-giving act. So many people have
never been heard in their whole lives.'

Joan Chittister OSB, *Called to Question: A Spiritual Memoir*
(London: Sheed and Ward, 2004), 123

Ω

'A father, a parent of three boys, once told me: "However bad
it gets, never cut off, never stop talking. My sons have done
most things. Keep listening, that's what I do." And listening
usually achieves more than giving advice.'

Jonathan Smith, *The Learning Game* (London: Little Brown and
Company, 2000), 222

Signpost—LISTENING IS PRODUCTIVE

A

'You have to listen to the river if you want to catch a trout.'

Irish Proverb

Ω

In July 2004 I heard Michael Frost, a fine speaker and lecturer at Morling College in Sydney, liken the ministry of teaching to that of the horse whisperer (as in the film and novel of the same name). Like horse whispering, teaching is about teasing out people's deepest yearnings.

Signpost—LISTENING AND CARING

A

'Spirituality is about listening, paying attention to the mystery in every moment.'

Michael Whelan SM

Ω

Good listeners are caring people. 'Care' comes from the Latin word *cura* meaning 'attention to, observance of'. Care is not about problem-solving. Care is learning to befriend problems.

'Honour the symptom and let it guide us in close care of the soul.'

Thomas Moore, *Care of the Soul: A Guide for Cultivating Depth and Sacredness in Everyday Life* (San Fransisco: HarperPerennial, 1994), 116

Signpost—LISTENING AND ENGAGEMENT WITH OTHERS

'Care' also comes from the gothic word *Kara* meaning 'mourning'. Care is a participation in the pain of another, a solidarity in suffering.

A

'Listeners are life's rarest breed . . . Listeners—those who hear the pain behind the pain . . . come few and far between.'

Joan Chittister OSB, *Called to Question: A Spiritual Memoir*, (London: Sheed and Ward, 2004), 124

Ω

'Cure without care is meaningless . . . Perhaps our problem has been too great a preoccupation with curing to the detriment of truly caring.'

Peter van Breemen, *Called by Name* (Denville, NJ: Dimension Books, 1976), 151

Signpost—GOOD LISTENING REQUIRES LISTENING TO OURSELVES

A

'Fifty years ago in 1949, the distinguished German theologian, Paul Tillich, wrote: "Most of our life continues on the surface. We are enslaved by the routine of our daily lives, in work, and pleasure, in business and recreation . . . We do not stop to look at the height above us, or to the depth below us . . . We talk and talk and never listen to the voices speaking to our depth and from our depth. We accept ourselves as we appear to ourselves, and do not care what we really are. Like hit and run drivers, we injure our souls by the speed with which we move on the surface; we miss, therefore, our depth and true life'."

Quoted in Professor Hedley Beare's speech night address to St Leonard's College in 1982 – already cited

Ω

'Writing is the way I think things through . . . "Writing . . . is a form of listening".'

Joan Chittister OSB, *Called to Question: A Spiritual Memoir* (London: Sheed and Ward, 2004), 9

'Be careful of words,
even the miraculous ones.
For the miraculous ones we do our best,
sometimes they swarm like insects
and leave not a sting but a kiss.
They can be good as fingers,
they can be trusty as the rock

you stick your bottom on.
But they can be both daisies and bruises.

Yet I am in love with words.
They are doves falling out of the ceiling.
They are six holy oranges sitting in my lap.
They are the trees, the legs of summer,
and the sun, its passionate face.

Yet often they fail me.
I have so much I want to say,
so many stories, images, proverbs, etc.
But the words aren't good enough,
the wrong ones kiss me.
Sometimes I fly like an eagle
but with the wings of a wren.

But I try to take care
and be gentle to them.
Words and eggs must be handled with care.
Once broken they are impossible
things to repair.'

Anne Sexton, 1928–1974, winner of the Pulitzer Prize

Signpost—LISTENING INVOLVES THE ART OF REFLECTION

A

'To encourage is to focus on assets and strengths and to minimise mistakes and deficiencies. Courage is by far the most important factor in growth and development, as individuals can become skilled or competent only when they believe in their own abilities to do so. Further, to have confidence in others, one must have confidence in oneself. Yet we constantly discourage young people by pointing out their mistakes and deficiencies in the mistaken belief that this will help them to develop. We have no confidence in others to improve by themselves and we do not trust our own ability to encourage them. The ability to encourage is the ability to instil self-confidence; this is by far the most important single quality which must be learned today.'

From a symposium paper in 1985 by Associate Professor Maurice Balson of Monash University

It is well worth reflecting on ourselves as parents and teachers concerning this role of encouragement. Do we encourage or discourage those entrusted to our care? In our own self-talk, do we encourage ourselves? Do we focus on our own negative qualities or our more plentiful, positive characteristics? It is valuable to listen to yourself from time to time—catch your words about others, to others, and listen to what you have to say to yourself, about yourself. Encouraging or discouraging?

Ω

'Like many precious commodities, the gift of time is difficult
to handle. Sometimes we have too much of it, more often too
little. Frequently we can hanker after the past or dwell on it
excessively—so much so that we forget that life is to be savoured
and enjoyed in the present. Similarly, we can wish our short lives
away so quickly that we live always for the future and miss out
on the beauties of the present time. We need to be reminded
that there is a place of rest in our lives, "a place where we must
be if we are to function well. This place of resting—the arms
of God, if you will—is simply here and now: seeing, hearing,
touching, smelling, tasting our life as it is".'

Stephanie Dowrick, *Forgiveness and Other Acts of Love: Finding True
Value in Your Life* (Sydney: Penguin, 1997). Quoting Zen teacher
Charlotte Joko Beck

Signpost—LISTENING AND SELF-KNOWLEDGE

Clearly, if self-knowledge is the platform for all successful leadership, we have to learn to pay attention and listen to the present moment in our lives. We need to become more aware of our thoughts, our feelings, our attitudes, and listen very carefully to what is happening within ourselves as we go about the ordinary business of daily life.

A

Eckhart Tolle captures these sentiments beautifully: 'The more you are focused on time—past and future—the more you miss the Now, the most precious thing there is. Why is it the most precious thing? Firstly, because it is the *only* thing. It's all there is. The eternal present is the space within which your whole life unfolds, the one factor that remains constant. Life is now. There was never a time when your life was *not* now, nor will there ever be. Secondly, the Now is the only point that can take you beyond the limited confines of the mind. It is your only point of access into the timeless and formless realm of Being.'

Eckhart Tolle, *The Power of Now: A Guide to Spiritual Enlightenment* (Novato, CA: New World Library, 1998)

Ω

The story is told of an old Cherokee warrior one evening telling his grandson about a battle that goes on inside all people. He said, 'My son, the battle is between two "wolves" inside us all. One is Evil. It is anger, envy, jealousy, sorrow, regret, greed, arrogance, self-pity, guilt, resentment, inferiority, lies, false pride, superiority, and ego. The other "wolf" is Good. It is joy, peace, love, hope, serenity, humility, kindness, benevolence, empathy, generosity, truth, compassion and faith.

His grandson thought about this story for a minute and then asked his grandfather: "Which wolf wins?" The old Cherokee warrior simply replied: "The one you feed".'

Signpost—LISTENING AND CONTEMPLATION

A

In this regard we have much to learn from our indigenous brothers and sisters who have the word 'dadirri' for that quality of deep listening. One Aboriginal woman, Miriam-Rose Ungunmerr-Baumann describes it this way: 'This is the gift that Australia is thirsting for. It is something like what you call "contemplation". A big part of "dadirri" is listening. Over the years, we have listened to our stories. They are told and and sung, over and over, as the seasons go on. As we grow older, we ourselves become the storytellers. We pass on to the young ones all they must know. "Dadirri" renews us and makes us whole. It is just being aware. My people are not threatened by silence. They are completely at home in it.'

Ω

'Loving God,
open our hearts,
so that we may feel the breath and play of your spirit.
Unclench our hands
so that we may reach out to one another,
and touch and be healed.
Open our lips
that we may drink in the delight and wonder of life.
Unclog our ears
to hear your agony in our inhumanity.
Open our eyes,
so that we may see Christ in friend and stranger.

Breathe your Spirit into us,
and touch our lives with the life of Christ,
Amen.'

Out of the Darkness: Paths to Inclusive Worship

From Margaret Hebblethwaite editor, *The Living Spirit—Prayers and Readings for the Christian Year: A Tablet Anthology* (London, 2000), 18

Signpost—LISTENING WITH MORE THAN OUR EARS

A

'To listen requires humility, for the thesis basic to listening is that others may quite possibly have something of value to say, something from which we can profit . . . But the talent for listening goes beyond listening with our ears. Really good listening also listens with the mind (and is, therefore, open and non-judgmental), with the heart (they are sensitive to their own and other people's emotional needs) the eyes (they know what to notice and what to overlook), and the touch (they sense when to reach out and when quietly to withdraw).'

Melannie Svoboda SND, 'Talents for Living in Community', in *Review For Religious*, January–February 1993, volume 52, number 1:131–139

Ω

'Whenever a student is at a critical moment of choice, when big decisions are to be made, or when they are on the point of making some sort of conversion (for example, in being reconciled with the school community after a serious behavioural lapse), I always ask them to spend some time reflecting on their experience and their way ahead. Invariably, I invite them to write me a letter. It is important to go to some lengths to convey that this is not a letter of apology, or an opportunity for me to see that they have done the right (expected?) thing on my terms. Rather, let them know that every life experience, positive or negative, is an opportunity for growth if reflected upon. There are no wasted experiences, however bad, if one can draw something from them in terms of self-awareness.'

Fr Ross Jones SJ, when Principal of Loyola Senior High
School, Mount Druitt, NSW

Signpost—REFLECTION IS ANOTHER FORM OF LISTENING

Reflection is the capacity to stop and ponder the meaning of one's experiences and the direction of one's life—to have the ability to place a mirror on one's actions and reflect back to oneself the value of one's activities.

A

Warren Bennis has written: 'Reflecting on experience means having a Socratic dialogue with yourself, asking the right questions at the right time, in order to discover the truth of yourself and your life . . . reflection is asking the questions that provide self-awareness beyond . . . reflection is a way of making learning conscious.'

The JSEA Bulletin, March, 1999

Ω

'Let every word
Be the fruit
Of action and reflection.
Reflection alone
Without action
Or tendency towards it
Is mere theory, adding its weight
When we are overloaded
With it already . . .
Action alone
Without reflection
Is being busy

Pointlessly.
Honour the Word eternal
And speak
To make
A new world possible.'

Dom Helder Camara *The Desert is Fertile*
(London: Sheed and Ward, 1974)

Signpost—LISTENING TO OUR OWN INTERNAL LANGUAGE

A

If I am to help others on their journeys, I must have this capacity for what Stephen Covey calls 'listening to my language'

'Ignatius of Loyola was a proud Spanish soldier who fought against the French in the battle of Pamplona in 1521 and suffered terrible injuries to his leg. During the painful months of convalescence, he spent a good deal of time daydreaming about the great deeds he would do as a knight and the beautiful ladies he would charm when he recovered. Deprived of any exciting reading material at Loyola Castle, he was offered the only books in the house—a copy of the life of Christ and a book on the Saints. Soon he found himself embarking on a second set of daydreams about how he could outdo the saints in their austerities for God. He noticed there was a difference between the two sorts of daydreams. After dreaming of his great military deeds and the ladies whose love he would win, he became bored, empty, and sad. Fantasising about outdoing the saints, however, led him to be happy, hopeful and encouraged. Reflecting on this qualitative difference, he started on a process which he was later to call the "Discernment of Spirits"—what we might term "sifting our moods and feelings" or "learning to read the body's signals". In brief, this is the *inside-out* of pastoral care—getting in touch with our inner life, which affects the way we perceive the world, act in it and react in it. We have to be able to sort out all those thoughts, memories, emotions, desires and fears, which are not random or meaningless. All of us have within us this alternation of moods—this contrast between positive and negative, light and dark, consolation and desolation, between the true and false self. Such self-learning becomes practical and fruitful when I obey the golden rule as a carer: good decisions can only come from the true self; bad decisions spring from the pressures and panics of the false self. Therefore never make a decision when "down". It is very important, therefore, to honour the symptoms of our own soul, to listen to the longings of our own hearts, if we are to be model carers for others.'

C Gleeson SJ, 'Affairs of the Heart: Quality of Soul in Our Relationships'
AHISA (Association of Heads of Independent Schools of Australia) Pastoral Care Conference—September 1996

Ω

'By being attentive, by learning to listen (or recovering the natural capacity to listen which cannot be learned any more than breathing), we can find ourself engulfed in such happiness that it cannot be explained: the happiness of being at one with everything in that hidden ground of Love for which there can be no explanations.'

Thomas Merton

From Margaret Hebblethwaite, editor, *The Living Spirit—Prayers and Readings for the Christian Year: A Tablet Anthology* (London, 2000), 280

Signpost—LISTENING AND FAITH

A

'The unexamined life is not worth living.'
Socrates

'I suspect that our age would counter with "the unlived life is not worth examining".'

Ronald Rolheiser, *Forgotten Among the Lilies: Learning to Love Beyond Our Fears* (New York: Doubleday, 2005), 126

Ω

'All the anxiety which arises in us when we ask "what can I do?" comes from the atheist part of ourselves. We are assuming that the real "I" is bounded by my own narrow and distorted vision of who I am. The real "I" is a unique manifestation of God in whom all things have their being. It is only when we can let go this narrow vision of "I" that we can begin to glimpse who we are, and it can only be a glimpse this side of death. "Unless you lose your life (the false sense of 'I'), you cannot find it (the true self, the Christ-self). We live in God. Faith is living in the awareness of this truth, recognizing God in the facts in which we live, letting him be God in our lives".'

Gerard W Hughes SJ, *Walk to Jerusalem: In Search of Peace* (London: DLT, 1991), 174

Signpost—LISTENING IS TUNING IN BEFORE TURNING IN

A

'Where have I been in spirit today? That's a good question for any Christian to ask oneself at the end of the day, by tuning in before turning in. The small details that I can so easily overlook can be rediscovered, maybe as big moments, certainly as precious ones. As I recall the day, when did I experience a deep peace, maybe even the peace that surpassed understanding. Maybe I can name its cause. Why, yes, I saw children full of delight and caught some of it for myself. For some reason I caught sight of the horizon over the paddocks or way out to sea, and its calmness came to me. I was walking, and the rhythm eased me. That music always does this to me. Thanks to that phone call, a cloud in my life lifted. Somehow my spirit became very still.

Sometimes there is not telling how, because the peace comes unbidden. I find myself bathed in peace. A sense of peace descends upon me. The well spring of delight is just there, welling up. Then the delight turns, almost automatically, to a sense of gratitude.

All this comes from attending to these experiences of being gifted, or graced, scattered through the day, mutely exploding.'

Andrew Bullen SJ, Rector of St Ignatius' College, Riverview, in
Viewpoint, 2005

Ω

'Learning about the tuning of one's own harp strings . . . is an
ongoing process . . .

Just as leadership demands a strategy of mobilising people,
it also requires a strategy of deploying and restoring one's own
spiritual resources.'

Ron Heifetz, *Leadership Without Easy Answers* (Cambridge Mass:
The Belknap Press, 1994)

Signpost—LISTENING IN THE HERE AND NOW

A

'I think you have to really reflect on what you are doing and
why you are doing it, to make it important, make it worthwhile
for yourself and for the people that you are teaching. When
you have made those connections and reflections for yourself,
it becomes real. Someone discusses it with you, a colleague
talks to you about it and you have a real sense of moving in the
same direction.'
Primary Teacher

Elizabeth Hartnell-Young, 'New Roles for Knowledge
Builders—What Teachers tell us about working in the 21st
Century', *IARTV Seminar Series*, October 2003, number 127, 15

Ω

'This week in my Philosophy classes with the Year 5 & 6
girls we have been discussing the concept of *time*—a concept
philosophers have grappled with for many a year. We discussed
Edmund Husserl's definition of time—*time is experienced as eternal
now, in a flow from the past to the future—like hearing a single note but
knowing it is part of a song. It is the "here" and the "now" that is the
important part of time* . . . One of the most destructive and negative
attitudes towards one's past is the attitude of regret—the desire
to go back in time and change things—the "if only" syndrome.
I love the phrase from Edith Piaf, *Je ne regrette rien,* so full of free
acceptance.

"I am the Alpha and the Omega. The beginning and the end."
Revelation 21:6.'

Jacqueline McCallum, Head of Loreto Junior School,
Kirribilli, Newsletter, 1 April 2005

Signpost—LISTENING AND ACCURACY

A

'Some years ago a Year 11 History student approached me with a request. He had been instructed to interview half a dozen adults about the history of the present century. One of the questions was: Who do you think are the six most significant world figures of the 20th century? Among others I nominated Lenin, the architect of the Russian Revolution. I regarded the Cold War, the reshaping of the political landscape, the build-up of nuclear missiles, etc as enough to justify the label "significant", whatever my personal opinion of Lenin. The young man then quizzed me in a rather puzzled way about Lenin's CV and obviously had doubts about my capacity for the accurate research required in a respectable history teacher. The confusion disappeared when I realised that, while I was talking about Vladimir Lenin, he thought I was referring to John Lennon, the Beatle. It was a healthy reminder that the cultural landscape does change and no educator can ignore the movement.'

Michael Stoney SJ, 'Nourishing Leaders for the Third Millennium', October 1996

Ω

Stethoscope inventor, RTH Laennec: 'Listen to your patients; they are telling you how to heal them.'

Signpost—LISTENING AND THE INNER WORLD OF STUDENTS

A

'Nothing separates and isolates people more effectively than language, and each world of youth has its own language. This is often indecipherable to those outside their world, and intentionally so. It is in part the reason why some ethnic groups deliberately keep their own language of their country of origin . . . *The language of the inner world* is imaginative, often secret and private. It is the language of beliefs, however irrational. It is the language of the personal diary, of poetry and above of all music and art. It is essentially the language of the creative mind. Increasingly it is also the habitat of mind altering drugs. Religions have long recognised that there is a specific language of the spiritual world . . .'

Dr John M Court, 'The Four Worlds of Youth'— a paper given to me by former Geelong Grammer School Deputy Head, Sean Burke

Ω

◆'A good teacher is like a candle—it consumes itself to light the way for others.'

Author unknown

Signpost—IN THE REALM OF THE SACRED

A

'As educators we deal with people's dreams—their individual and personal visions—and because of this, every day we are in the realm of the sacred. We are involved with forces and energies larger than our own. We are engaged in a sacred transaction of which we know only a little: we see the shadow, never the shape.'

Ruth Stuart Starratt, 'Education with a Sense of Wonder: A Spiritual Journey', in *Catholic Education: A Journal of Inquiry and Practice*, volume 3, number 2, December 1999: 216–225

Ω

◆ 'Teaching has an extraordinary moral depth and is one of many most excellent and creative activities, for the teacher does not write on inanimate material, but on the very spirit of human beings.'

Congregation for Catholic Education
Quoted in a paper by Robert Fitzgerald 'Catholic Schools and Justice: A Counter Cultural Agenda', Paper to Catholic School Leaders, Parramatta CEO (Catholic Education Office), 29 February 2000

Signpost—LISTENING FOR THE TRUTH

A

'We must ask ourselves whether we are nurturing the idea of truth as correctness, of having the right construct, or truth as a mode of being. I suspect that a very good test of whether a lesson has gone well would be to ask: did I look on my students in light and love? . . This is the difference, and it is an important difference, between teaching in order to instruct, and teaching in order to enlighten.'

Felicity, McCutcheon, 'Truth in the Bible', Paper delivered at the *Dialogue Australasia Network* Conference, Adelaide, 2004

Ω

'For this reason there is a close link between truth and love. This may seem strange, since we usually think of love as a nice warm feeling and nothing to do with the mind. But loving another person includes trying to understand who he or she really is. Growing in love implies coming to understand them, see through their eyes, penetrate their humanity; and growth in understanding overflows in love. Our contemporaries tend to think of knowledge as cold, an impersonal detachment, observing a distance. The Bible suggests otherwise: the word "know" means a most intimate, indeed a sexual, relationship. Knowledge implies intimacy. Love helps me to know the truth, and the truth helps me to love.'

Timothy Radcliffe OP, *I Call You Friends* (London: Continuum, London, 2003), 80

Signpost—LISTENING TO CREATION

A

'You can't call yourself a Catholic until you've wondered why God doesn't send e-mail. After all, God does have a Web site. It's called creation. Creation has links to everything. All God's most personal details are there on the Web site, if you know how to look. The church is supposed to be God's search engine. It is meant to help us find our way around the Web site.

God does not send e-mail because God is merciful. And wise. God knows there is too much e-mail happening already. Once upon a time, people began a day at the office with a cup of coffee and a quick chat about the news and traffic. There is not time left for such niceties. Workers now have to get down to the pressing task of deleting from their computers the overnight accumulation of spam.

When you think about it, spam is a bit like grace. Nobody knows where it comes from or why. But the minute you make the slightest response, you get a whole lot more.

The difference is that grace is helpful.'

Michael McGirr, 'Wonderful Spam! Lovely Spam! Eternal Spam!', in *NCR*, 14 January 2005

Ω

'If you have a thousand reasons for living,
If you never feel alone
If you wake up wanting to sing,
If everything speaks to you,
From the stone in the road
To the star in the sky,

From the loitering lizard
To the fish, lord of the sea,
If you understand the winds
And listen to the silence,
Rejoice, for God walks with you,
He is your comrade, is your brother!'

Dom Helder Camara

Signpost—LISTENING REQUIRES HUMILITY

A

'The last six years afforded me much time and food for thought. I came to the conclusion that the human race is not divided into two opposing camps of good and evil. It is made up of those who are capable of learning and those who are incapable of doing so . . . As we strive to teach others we must have the humility to acknowledge that we too have much to learn.'

Aung San Suu Kyi

Ω

The following card has been given to all students at St Aloysius' College in Sydney as something they might keep in their wallets to help them develop the Ignatian habit of reflective listening.

The Alo's 5 Stars
Under the Southern Cross
Being aware of God's presence today . . .
1. What was the best thing I heard?
2. What was the best thing I saw?
3. What was the best thing someone did for me?
4. What was the best thing I did for someone else?
5. What can I do to improve tomorrow?
Thank you God

Signpost—OBEDIENCE IS DEEP LISTENING

A

'Many commentators have said that the contemporary Catholic church is divided along ideological lines, between the so-called "progressives" and "conservatives". What would Benedict's advice be to Benedict XVI, as he confronts such a reality? In one beautiful phrase Benedict said that the leader of the community 'must so arrange everything that the strong have something to yearn for and the weak nothing to run from.

Benedict upholds obedience as a key virtue. But this obedience is not a mindless submissiveness, rather a deep listening for the voice of the Spirit at work within the individual and the community. The first word of Benedict's Rule is "Listen". All members of the community and the leader in particular, are to listen "with the ear of the heart."'

Sr Patty Fawkner SGS, formerly Director of Uniya and a
Sister of the Good Samaritan of the Order of St Benedict,
'What's in a Name?'—a talk in April 2005 given as the new
Pope Benedict XVI assumed office

Ω

'When we can be with what is, we can find peace, joy, even
bliss, in our everyday lives . . . "All the way to heaven is
heaven", said Saint Catherine of Siena. We need to surrender
to the happiness that is found in being with what is.'

Terence Grant, *The Silence of Unknowing: The Key to the Spiritual
Life* (Missouri: Ligouri, 1995), 4

Signpost—AUTHORITY COMMANDS CAREFUL LISTENING

A

'After hearing about 150 piano renditions of the same song by five-year old contestants at the City arts festival, I had endured about all I could bear. Finally, it was time to find out who could win. The atmosphere was emotionally charged, and I wondered how the judge would be able to choose a winner without causing a riot.

The parents and children gathered for the announcement, and the judge was introduced. From his first word, I was hooked. The crowd calmed down as he spoke, for here was a person who knew what he was talking about. He spoke warmly about the children, about the wonder of music, about the importance of encouraging love of music at an early age. He had a quiet and unmistakable authority. He made music the real winner.

This man's obvious authority and love for his subject made me think of how Jesus must have affected his hearers. The teaching of Jesus fell upon receptive ears because he was someone who spoke with love and authority. When we listen carefully to Jesus' words, we know he is talking to us and that he is talking about what really matters. Those who listen have their whole lives changed.'

Bill Adams, Queensland, Australia

Ω

'Happiness is a journey, not a destination.

Work like you don't need money,
Love like you've never been hurt,
And dance like noone's watching.'

Signpost—TOUCHING THE HEART

A

'He will have to learn, I know, that all people are not just, all people are not true,
But teach him also that for every scoundrel there is a hero,
That for every selfish politician, there is a dedicated leader.

Teach him that for every enemy there is a friend.
Teach him to learn to lose and also to enjoy winning.
Steer him away from envy, if you can.
Teach him the secret of quiet laughter.
Teach him the wonder of books; but also give him quiet time
To ponder the eternal mystery of birds in the sky, bees in the sun,
And flowers on a green hillside.

In school teach him it is far more honourable to fail than to cheat.
Teach him to have faith in his own ideas,
Even if everyone tells him they are wrong.
Teach him to be gentle with gentle people and tough with the tough.
Try to give him the strength not to follow the crowd when everyone is getting on the bandwagon.
Teach him to listen to all people, but teach him also to filter all he hears on a screen of truth, and take only the good that comes through.
Teach him to close his ears to a howling mob; and to stand and fight if he thinks he's right.
Teach him gently, but do not coddle him; as only the test of fire makes fine steel.

Let him have the courage to be impatient, let him have the
patience to be brave.
Teach him always to have sublime faith in his Creator and
faith in himself too, because then he will always have faith in
humanity.
This is a big order, but please see what you can do.
He is such a fine little fellow, my son.'

Abraham Lincoln about his son . . . to the Headmaster

Ω

'I have a theory that only what touches the heart is really
lodged in the mind. Memory is made up of what has touched
our lives
. . . It is time, I think, to release feeling into the world.'

Joan Chittister OSB, *Called to Question: A Spiritual Memoir*
(London: Sheed and Ward, 2004), 152

Signpost—ACTIVE LISTENING AND OBEDIENCE

A

'Obedience is active listening for the movement of the spirit
in every moment, everywhere; obedience hears, sees, feels and
becomes imbued with Being beyond mere seeming; obedience
yearns to submit to the ways of the Community of Love we
call God.'

Catalyst Suggestion Sheet number 37

Ω

'Hindu India developed a lovely image to describe the
relationship between God and his Creation. God "dances" his
creation. He is the Dancer, his creation is the Dance.
. . . Be silent and look at the Dance. Just look: a star, a flower, a
fading leaf, a bird, a stone . . . Any fragment of the Dance will
do. Look. Listen. Smell. Touch. Taste. And, hopefully, it won't
be long before you see Him—the Dancer Himself.'

Anthony De Mello SJ, *The Song of the Bird* (Gujurat, India,
1982), 16

'This year we seem to have been talking and thinking a good
deal about dance. "Dancing with the Stars" has been a very
popular television program, so it has been interesting to hear
Richard Rohr describe the Trinity as the Dance of God. For
many centuries Hindu India has developed a beautiful image to
describe the relationship between God and His creation. They
talk about God "dancing" his creation. God is the Dancer, and
His creation is the Dance. While the dance is different from

the dancer, it has no existence apart from Him. In *Gift from the Sea*, Ann Morrow Lindbergh likens a good relationship to a good dance. "Lightness of touch and living in the moment are intertwined. One cannot dance well unless one is completely in time with the music, not leaning back to the last step or pressing forward to the next one, but poised directly on the present step as it comes. Perfect poise on the beat is what gives good dancing its sense of ease, of timelessness, of the eternal".'

C Gleeson SJ, 'Try to be Here', in *Madonna*,
November-December, 2006

Somewhere in his voluminous writings Michael Fallon MSC tells the story of one his students talking about the Trinity as the Dance of God. The Father is the Dance; the Son is the Dancer; and the Holy Spirit is the Dancing.

Signpost—GOD WINKING AT US DURING THE DAY

A

'It was fascinating as a religious person to hear a couple of years ago on national radio in Sydney a guest speaker on the afternoon "Drive Time" show talking about God "winking at you" during the day. Petria King was making the point that one of the great blessings of our body is that it is always in the present, in the world of what is. If one believes in God, the present is where He can be found. The mind, on the other hand, with its endless inner commentary, tries to take us off into the future, into the world of what isn't. Creativity is a present time activity, and if we are absent from the present we sacrifice the following four qualities of our lives: our spontaneity; our humour; our creativity; and our self-confidence.

Clearly, if self-knowledge is the platform for all successful leadership, we have to learn to pay attention and listen to the present moment in our lives. We need to become more aware of our thoughts, our feelings, our attitudes, and listen very carefully to what is happening within ourselves as we go about the ordinary business of daily life.'

C Gleeson SJ, talk to the CSA (Q) Conference, July 2004

Ω

'The laughter of human beings must correspond to something
in God. He shares our sorrows: he must also share our
laughter, so I prayed to recognize the wink of God and to hear
his laughter in my own and other people's seriousness and
solemnity.'

G Hughes, *Walk to Jerusalem, op cit*, 135

Signpost—LISTENING TO OURSELVES

A

'At the very end of George Bernanos' classic French novel *Diary of a Country Priest*, which depicts the corruption and excesses of the Church of the day, the good and honest young curate is dying of painful stomach cancer. His friend, who is with him, has sent for the Priest to administer the last rites and they are waiting for him to arrive. The friend writes:

> The priest was still on his way, and finally I was bound to voice my deep regret that such a delay threatened to deprive my comrade of the final consolation of the church . . . He then uttered these words . . . And I am quite sure that I have recorded them accurately, for his voice, though halting, was strangely distinct: *Does it matter? Grace is everywhere . . .* '

C Gleeson SJ, Talk to Xavier College Staff, 27 January 2000

Ω

'To cultivate quality of soul in others, we need to have some time for our own souls. Professor Ron Heifetz of Harvard University speaks about the need for having a balcony in our lives if we are to understand the sometimes frenzied dance of events going on around us. Without such a balcony, we can easily be swept up in the dance of life and lose our perspective. Where is the balcony for my soul? In order to keep perspective on all the events going on around us every day—the dance of life—we need to be able to get to the balcony to see all the patterns of movement on the dance floor. To interpret events, spiritual leaders need to understand their own ways of processing and distorting what they hear. What we have termed discernment of spirits or the art of reflection, Heifetz writes in similar fashion: "Learning about the tuning of one's own harpstrings, how one is inclined to resonate more with certain themes than with others, is an ongoing process . . . Just as leadership demands a strategy of mobilising people, it also requires a strategy of deploying and restoring one's own spiritual resources" (Ron Heifetz, *Leadership Without Easy Answers* (Cambridge: Harvard Belknap).'

C Gleeson SJ, ACEL Talk, Hobart, 6 July 2004

Signpost—HAVE WE HEARD FROM OURSELVES TODAY?

A

'The American author Thoreau wrote once: "When our life ceases to be inward and private, conversation degenerates into mere gossip . . . In proportion as our inward life fails, we go more constantly and desperately to the post office. You may depend on it, that the poor fellow who walks away with the greatest number of letters proud of his extensive correspondence has not heard from himself this long while." Have we heard from ourselves lately? We need to cultivate, quite deliberately, the daily habit of silence.'

Quoted in H Beare's Address to the 1982 Upper School
Speech Night at St Leonard's College, Brighton.

Ω

All spirituality is, in one sense or another, about transformation or even transcendence. WH Auden once wrote: 'To pray is to pay attention to something or someone other than oneself. Whenever a man so concentrates his attention—on a landscape, a poem, a geometrical problem, an idol, or the True God—that he completely forgets his own ego and desires, he is praying.'

Signpost—LISTENING IN CLASS TIME

A

'I also use periods of silence in the middle of a class, especially in an open discussion when the words start to tumble out upon each other and the problem we are trying to unravel is getting more tangled. I try to help my students learn to spot those moments and settle into a time of quiet reflection in which the knots might come untied. We need to abandon the notion that "nothing is happening" when it is silent, to see how much new clarity a silence often brings.'

Parker Palmer, *To Know as We Are Known A: Spirituality Education* (San Francisco: HarperCollins, 1983, 1993), 80

'Surely cultivating an appreciation of silence in a world haunted by noise pollution is worthwhile.'

Bob Slattery SJ, *Integral Pedagogy* (Education Through Process Rather than Content)

Ω

'We listen to our students. As someone has said, God gave us one mouth and two ears to remind us that we must listen twice as much as we speak.'

Melannie Svoboda SND, *Teaching is like Peeling Back Eggshells* (Mystic CT: Twenty-third Publications, 1994)

Signpost—LISTENING TO GOD'S CREATION

A

'Love all God's creation,
The whole and every grain of sand in it.
Love every leaf, every ray of God's light.
Love the animals, love the plants, love everything.
If you love everything,
You will perceive the divine mystery in things.
Once you perceive it,
You will begin to comprehend it better every day.
And you will come at last to love the whole world
With an all-embracing love.'

Feodor Dostoevski

Ω

'If you have a thousand reasons for living,
If you never feel alone,
If you wake up wanting to sing,
If everything speaks to you,
From the stone in the road
To the star in the sky,
From the loitering lizard
To the fish, lord of the sea,
If you understand the winds
And listen to the silence,
Rejoice, for God walks with you,
He is your comrade, is your brother!'

Dom Helder Camara

Signpost—LISTENING TO GOD ALL AROUND US

A

'In the story of Emmaus, Jesus leads the disciples to discover
him both in the Scriptures and in the act of offering
hospitality to a stranger. I interpret this to mean that God
seeks us through the stranger, and while this means allowing
people I think I know well—my husband of twenty years, for
example—to be a stranger, his own mysterious self that I will
never fully comprehend, it also means being willing to be fully
present to the strangers I meet.'

Kathleen Norris in *How Can I Find God?*, edited by James
Martin (Missouri: Ligouri, 1997), 178

Ω

'I have come to understand that the voice of God is all
around me. God is not a silent God. God is speaking to me
All the time. In everything. Through everyone. I am only now
beginning to listen, let alone to hear. In bare trees, I hear God
saying that it is possible to die over and over again and yet
survive. In the stones of this Irish landscape I hear God saying
that there is nothing that can't be endured. Not the storm, not
the wind, not even the passage of time.'

Joan Chittister OSB, *Called to Question: A Spiritual Memoir*
(London: Sheed and Ward, 2004), 185

'And God said:
May you delight in your body.
It is my body too.

May you see the world anew each day:
How else can I behold my beauty?
May you fill the earth with the sounds of life:
How else can I hear my song?

May your skin rejoice in the passion of the sun;
And your tongue tingle with the joy of new wine.
Don't you know you are my senses? Without your body
I cannot be.'

Daniel J O'Leary, *Travelling Light: Your Journey to Wholeness*, (Dublin: The Columba Press, 2001), 30

Teaching and Storytelling

PREVIEW WINDOW

One of my more attentive students once asked me why I always began my Homilies with a story. 'Not that I mind, Father, I am just curious', he added hastily. I tried to explain that stories act as a bridge to our audience or congregation, and immediately link the listener to the speaker's experience. We are born into a community of storytellers, our family, and we grow up listening to stories from a very young age. Stories that reveal the best qualities of the human spirit and character connect us immediately to God and tell us something about Him or Her. The best teachers excel in storytelling and imitate God, the supreme storyteller, in doing so.

Signpost—GOD THE SUPREME STORYTELLER

A

Susan Ohanian (1989) once observed:
'The more I teach, the more I realise that we teachers are
    nothing but our anecdotes, our reflections on experience.
        As teachers, we become the stories we choose to tell.'

Teaching and storytelling are ennobled because they are part of
    God's work as the supreme weaver of stories.

Ω

'That same day, Jesus left the house and sat by the lakeside, but
    such crowds gathered round him that he got into a boat and
sat there. The people all stood on the beach, and he told them
                many things in parables.'

Matthew 13:1–3

Signpost—GOD LOVES STORIES

A

Elie Wiesel, the great Jewish author, has written that 'God made man because he loves stories'.

from *The Gates of the Forest*

Ω

'There is something more to be said about "telling the story". The hearer of the story becomes with the teller a shared caretaker of the story. That is true of the family story and the school story, just as it is of the sacred story. Stories create conditions of empathy and they allow empathy to be given without ideological or theological interference.'

Peter W Cobb, 'Teachers as a Rainbow Tribe', Keynote Address at the AARE-CSEE Conference, July 2002

Signpost—STORIES BRIDGE THE SACRED AND SECULAR

A

'Whether sung or told, stories are themselves thresholds for stepping from the profane into the sacred . . . All children, I think, need to have faith that some things are sacred, that not all is profane, that some things endure, that not everything is transient, that some things have authority, that not all authority is corrupt, that there is transcendent purpose, that not all meaning falls to and on the self.'

Peter Cobb, as above

Ω

'In the first place, we should be endeavouring to help young people tell their stories, thereby nurturing in them the life of the imagination. When we think about it, stories are a very important part of our whole life. We are born into a community of story-tellers—our family—and take on their story even before we see the light of day. If we are fortunate enough to have had a strong family life, we will have had stories told and read to us from a very early age. If we have the good fortune to belong to a school community with strong history and tradition, we will have been immersed again and again in all its stories and myths. Stories, as William Bausch points out, are a bridge to our roots. They provide meaning and coherence in helping us relate to our world. We tell stories to make sense of our experience and, in the telling, we ourselves are told.'

C Gleeson SJ, *Dorothy Knox Lecture*, 2002

Signpost—OUR STORY IS SACRED GROUND

A

'In her highly successful radio program of interviews over eight years—*The Search for Meaning*—Caroline Jones came to the recognition "that a person's experience, their story, is sacred ground, that it's essential to them, that they're lost without it, that it needs to be told, and, importantly, to be heard". Every story demands a listener, and to listen to a person's story and understand the unexpressed questions and yearnings contained therein, requires that we believe in the uniqueness and importance of each story, of each individual life. Many young people, however, are afraid to tell their story because they think that it is neither clever nor beautiful. No one would want to hear it. Because "storytelling is an excellent way of caring for the soul", we must find ways of slicing through this natural reluctance to tell one's story.'

C Gleeson SJ, *Dorothy Knox Lecture*, 2002

Ω

Cardinal John Henry Newman understood the crucial importance of imagination for developing our faith, arguing over a century ago: ' . . . the heart is commonly reached, not through the reason, but through the imagination.' Belief in God, he says, originates in our imagination, not in any ideas. The real battles of life take place within the imagination.

Signpost—STORIES TOUCH THE HEART

A

'I have arrived at most of my conclusions in life through feeling and through experience rather than through sustained thought. Love of words, yes, habits of enquiry, yes, hours of application, yes, but it all had to go hand in hand with the human dimension: it needed heart. I wanted my children to feel the concerns of the heart just as much as I wanted them to cut to the heart of the matter.'

Jonathan Smith, *The Learning Game: A Teacher's Inspirational Story*
(London: Little, Brown, and Company, 2000), 13

Ω

'Thomas Moore claims that "we are condemned to live out what we cannot imagine". Through the imagination, a person "reconstructs past experience and is able to give a verdict on his or her self and life". Telling our story, particularly in the presence of a careful listener, will reveal those images responsible for attitudes of discouragement and confusion, or emotions of fear, depression, and resentment. It will help us find a sequence and pattern in our life; to order events is itself an act of judgment. In all stories there are "discoveries, revelations, and surprises in the telling: gifts of grace now forgotten, wounds not yet healed, goals and desires persisting over many years". Stories are clearly an important avenue to developing the life of the imagination.'

C Gleeson SJ, 'Quality of Soul—Spirituality in Schools',
Dialogue Australia, November, 2001, Thomas Moore, *Care
of the Soul*, and Kathleen Fischer, *The Inner Rainbow: The
Imagination in Christian Life*

Signpost—TEACHER AS KEEPER OF THE DREAM

A

'In ancient times according to legends the King or Queen placed the Keeper of Dreams beside the throne to retell the ancient stories of the people and nurture their dreams. A teacher can be a "dream keeper" for students by fostering their hopes about future possibilities and challenging them to dream the impossible dream. Their dream should include how they want to use their life and their education, to contribute to the common good and to serve others and work for justice.'

Sr Pat Murray IBVM, 'Daring to be an Educator', a talk at the Loreto Schools Network Day, 22 November, 1997

Ω

'All of us in schools are in competition for the hearts of our young people with a variety of image-makers in the rock world and the consumer society. We have to capture their imaginations. If Irish Jesuit author Michael Paul Gallagher, *Struggles of Faith* (Dublin: The Columba Press, Dublin, 1991), 78, is right that "apathy is often the face of hurt hope, or hidden hunger", then it is our task in schools to provide better images of hope for our young people. How can we do that?'

C Gleeson SJ, '*Quality of Soul': Spirituality in Schools,* an article for *Dialogue Australia,* November, 2001

Signpost—IMAGINATION ESSENTIAL FOR FAITH

A

'CS Lewis tells the story of his conversion in a little autobiographical piece entitled "Surprised by Joy". His journey has some things to teach us.

For years he was blocked from committing himself to faith precisely because of his keen, uncompromising intellect. Brilliant, searching, sceptical of easy answers, he was unable to picture to himself how the great events of Christ's life and resurrection could have happened.

Moreover, he saw commitment to faith as somehow selling short one's freedom. In all of this, he was constantly challenged by JRR Tolkien, the author of *The Lord of the Rings*, a friend and a practising Roman Catholic. Lewis recalls how, on many an evening, Tolkien and he would have dinner together and then walk the streets of Oxford for hours, arguing faith and religion.

On one such evening, shortly before his conversion, Tolkien challenged him to this effect: "Your inability to picture for yourself the mysteries of Jesus' life is a failure of imagination on your part". Lewis was stung by that remark, but realised too its truth.'

Ron Rolheiser OMI, 'True and False Notions of Freedom', *Tidings Online*, 11 August 2003

Ω

'The language of God is the experience God writes into our lives.'

St John of the Cross

Signpost—OUR STORIES AS LIFE MAPS

A

'In her splendid closing Address to the 2001 American National Catholic Education Association Conference, Sister Joan Chittister OSB told the following story about cartographers in 1635 publishing their maps of California as an island. When the missionaries arrived there and discovered that California was part of the mainland, they wrote home to the cartographers and the Crown to say that California was not an island. No one believed them. Indeed, in 1701 almost 70 years later, the officials reissued an updated version of the same map! Those using the coastline for all of that time assumed that the data of their maps had the inerrancy of tradition. Finally, in 1721, the heretics and rebels won out and the official maps attached California to the mainland. It therefore took "almost a hundred years for the gap between experience and authority to close" and "for the new maps to be declared official, despite the fact that the people who were there all the time knew differently from the very first day".

In using this story Sister Joan was making the point that "the truth is always larger than the partial present".'

C Gleeson SJ, Opening the 2001 AHISA (Association of Heads of Independent Schools of Australia) Conference in Sydney

Ω

'Novelist Bruce Chatwin writes about the Aboriginal belief in song-lines in his book of the same name: "Each totemic ancestor, while traveling through the country, was thought to have scattered a trail of words and musical notes along the line of his footprints, and . . . these Dreaming-tracks lay over the land as 'ways' of communication between the most far-flung tribes. A Song', Arkady said, 'was both map and direction-finder.' Providing you knew the song, you could always find your way across the country. 'And would a man on "Walkabout" always be travelling down one of the Songlines?' 'Yes!'."

'These Songlines represent the wisdom and knowledge of the ancestors as they crossed the great continent and sang the world into existence. And so the Aboriginal people believe that each person must go and find the right songline, to connect with the ancestors and to continue singing up the country. I believe that education can be that kind of experience especially when it helps each young person to begin a life journey of response to the questions "what was I born to be and to do?" Each person has a songline to find and the opportunity to make concrete what is already potentially present within them. I often say to students "go out and find your songline, sing the world into being, rid it of injustice and oppression, transform relationships across all the barriers that divide us. Go and find your songline—if not our world will be the poorer without your song.".'

Sr Pat Murray, 'Daring to be an Educator', a talk given at the
Loreto Schools' Network Day, 22 November 1997

Signpost—GOOD LITERATURE AND IMAGINATION

A

'I am sure all keen watchers of (current) trends in Higher School Certificate English could resonate easily with the British author of an article entitled "the strange death of literate England" when he wrote: "The study of literature in schools and universities has taken a different turn. Interest is focused sometimes on ideological content: is the work tainted with colonialist attitudes? Is it subtly misogynist? What does it tell us about the struggles of its time? All literature, we hear from some influential quarters, is about power." This is a far cry from the magnificent perspective on literature offered by CS Lewis: "Literature enlarges our being by admitting us to experiences not our own. They may be beautiful, terrible, awe-inspiring, exhilarating, pathetic, comic, or merely piquant. Literature gives the entree to them all. Those of us who have been true readers all our life, seldom fully realise the enormous extension of our being which we owe to authors . . . In reading good literature, I become a thousand men, and yet remain myself. Like the night sky in a Greek poem, I see with a myriad eyes, but it is still I who see. Here, as in worship, in love, in moral action, and in knowing, I transcend myself; and am never more myself than when I do."

Is not that a splendid quote about literature? "Here . . . I transcend myself, and am never more myself than when I do". I believe there is a real hunger for the spiritual in our school communities which remains largely untapped.'

C Gleeson SJ, Opening 2001 AHISA (Association of Heads of Independent Schools of Australia) Conference

Ω

'From the moment Ann Clark crossed the Duck River in January 1987, a sense of excitement was felt in the schools in the fast growing diocese.

Among her many gifts, Ann was known for her great flair and a wonderful sense of occasion and the fact that she was never afraid to try something that had not been tried before.

She was fearless.

It was obvious she enjoyed the job. This was most evident when she was visiting schools. She frequently spoke about what the students had told her. Her gift of communication with students, I'm sure, sometimes made principals nervous!

While visiting a primary classroom, one occasion, she was engaging the children in conversation, as only Ann could, and thought she was making a great impression, as the much heralded and important visitor of the day, when a bright-eyed child looked up and exclaimed knowingly "I know who you are".

Knowing the Principal had thoroughly drilled the children about her visit, Ann replied "Do you?" "You tell me then" and the response came quickly: "You're Father's Mother."

Ann was not so impressed with this response given that the Parish Priest was well over 70! Ann loved to relate these experiences. She sometimes referred to them as "moments of grace".'

Excerpt from Brother Kelvin Canavan's eulogy at the Mass of Thanksgiving for the life of Dr Ann Clark, Director of Catholic Education in the Parramatta Diocese, in January 1997

Signpost—STORIES AND IMAGINATION ENLARGE OUR LIVES

A

'In his autobiography, *The Quest for Grace* one time Melbourne Grammar student and eminent Australian historian Manning Clark talked about the different teachers he had experienced as a young man—distinguishing between those people he termed "life-straiteners" and those who were for him "life-enlargers", between those people who have a very measured, narrow view of life and want to contain it, and those who love the banquet of life with a passion and want to share it with others.

To be a "life enlarger" is surely the aspiration of all teachers and educators. If we look back on our own lives as students, I am sure we can identify our best teachers as those who were "life enlargers" for us.'

C Gleeson SJ, After Dinner speech to Xavier-Melbourne Grammar Staff, 27 August 2004

Ω

'The capacity to imagine a better world is a precious asset. I can remember the sadness of hearing adolescent psychologist Michael Carr Gregg speaking about some of the young people he counselled saying to him: "If I am not here, my problems are not here." In the same vein, author Thomas Moore in his book, *Care of the Soul* has penned those very stark words: "We are condemned to live out what we cannot imagine.".'

C Gleeson SJ, Xavier-Melbourne Grammar Staff, speech as above

Signpost—STORIES CHALLENGE OUR COMFORT ZONES

A

'When reading a 2003 Report on young adults involved in the Edmund Rice network, I noted the following words of its author, Peter Nicholson:

> On a cold Sunday morning in a bush setting south of Perth I listened to a group of young adults talking with great honesty and intensity about their lives. They spoke about their dreams, their hopes and their search for how best to live as human beings. They talked in a way that I or my contemporaries could never have done. I asked how the Congregation of the Christian Brothers and the Edmund Rice network might help them.
>
> Amongst the replies, not the first, were the words, "take us beyond our comfort zone". All of us need to be taken beyond our comfort zone. That is where we find human growth and human authenticity. That is where we find love, justice and community. That is where we find hope for ourselves and our world. That is where we find our God. Jesus looked at the rich young man with compassion and invited him to move beyond the comfort zone of his current lifestyle.

Imagination is the eye of the soul and is crucial in taking us beyond our comfort zones. Imagination asks "what's possible?", whereas technology asks "what works?" As Joan Chittister has said: "Imagination breaks open the human mind to what is desirable when what is real is unbearable." Teachers are by their very nature storytellers, and good story telling and story hearing are so important for developing a healthy imagination. Caroline

Jones is absolutely right in saying that "a person's experience, their story, is sacred ground.'"

C Gleeson SJ, Xavier-Melbourne Grammar Staff, speech as above

Ω

'As human beings we need to locate ourselves in stories. We need to have a sense of: "Once upon a time." We need to have a sense of "And they lived . . ." if not "and they lived happily ever after". Young people without this context of story have little reason for hope.'

C Gleeson SJ, Xavier-Melbourne Grammar Staff, speech as above

Signpost—STORIES REVEAL MORE THAN MEETS THE EYE

A

'*Once upon a time* . . . Sometimes children enter the world of the imagination cuddled up to a trusted adult reading them stories. At other times they enter that world alone, with books and fantasies as companions on this delightful journey. With experience, children learn that stories reveal more than meets the eye—that for example, stories of the past may illuminate the present. Stories may carry the wisdom of other cultures . . . They invite their listeners and readers, young and old, to enter a fabulous world in which feelings can be aroused, characters understood and events explored, all within the safe boundaries of the beginning and the ending. Children learn that even threatening experiences can be explored through imagination, safe in the knowledge that there will always be a resolution to a good story.'

Roslyn Arnold, *Empathic Intelligence: Teaching, Learning, Relating* (Sydney: UNSW Press, 2005), 63, 64

Ω

'In telling our own stories, we feel an affinity with our past and in hearing the stories of others we can feel an affinity with them. Storylines connect individuals across time and space. They can inspire the young and affirm the old, providing imagined role models for all kinds of endeavours, while reminding us that experience endures beyond our own mortality.'

Roslyn Arnold, *Empathic Intelligence, op cit,* 71

Signpost—STORIES HELP US TO IMAGINE A BETTER WORLD

A

'For some deeply engaged readers, stories herald moments of private intimacy, and from such experience in our inner world grows the capacity for empathy, imagination, creativity, playful and moral conjecturing about it. "I wonder what it would be like to be the strongest girl in the world?" "What would I do if I were held captive in a castle surrounded by fire-breathing dragons?" Or more realistically: "How would I respond if I were tempted with fame and fortune as reward for a favour or some secret information?".'

Roslyn Arnold, *Empathic Intelligence, op cit*, 71, 72

Ω

'Our capacity as humans to imagine a better world is a precious asset. The content, shape, feel of that world is capable of being brought to life by a richly sourced imagination. Formal education has enormous potential to source this precious asset. Calling on the power of the microscope, breaking open the text of a Shakespearian play, accessing the thoughts and feelings of another culture/language are just a few of the possibilities open to educators in this area of the imagination. One of the most powerful examples in my own experience was to set for study by my Year 12 Literature class a slim volume of three plays by Athol Fugard, a South African playwright. The plays dealt variously with the passbook situation, in *Sizwe Bansi is Dead*, the prison experience, in *The Island* and the infamous Immorality Act outlawing sexual relationships between blacks and other racial groups. None of us in that class would ever be able to experience personally what it was to be black and living under apartheid. But I can guarantee that these plays left an indelible impression and a level of understanding in those girls that no amount of political comment could match. By calling on the imagination, literature offers the opportunity of vicarious experience—maybe life at one remove but definitely life and to a depth unimagined.'

Deirdre Rofe IBVM, 'Education and Social Conscience',
Jesuit Lenten Series of Lectures 1999 (Melbourne: Jesuit
Publications, 1999), 271, 272

Signpost—STORIES HELP US TO DREAM AND SHARE GOD'S DREAM

A

'Storytelling has ancient roots, going back to when we were more connected to our communities, to the great "unknown". They improve our ability to listen, to speak, to create our own stories, to *imagine*. In folk and fairy tales people go on wondrous adventures. Elves, sprites or animals help them along the way just when all looks lost.

"Come to the edge", he said. They said, "We are afraid".
"Come to the edge", he said.
They came. He pushed them, and they flew . . .'

Guillaume Apollinaire

'Stories give us a different way of perceiving the world, one where optimism reigns, where if you put your courage to the sticking place, if you follow your heart's desire, you'll be likely to fly.'

Andrew McKenna, 'Swimming through Dreams'

Ω

'And the Lord God said,

"I myself will dream a dream within you.
Good dreams come from me you know!
My dreams seem impossible—
not too practical, not for the cautious man or woman—
a little risky sometimes.

A trifle brash perhaps.
Some of my friends prefer to rest more comfortably
in sounder sleep with visionless eyes.
But for those who share my dream −
I ask a little patience, a little humour, some small courage, and
a LISTENING heart.
I will do the rest.
Then they will risk, and wonder at their daring,
run, and marvel at their speed,
build, and stand in awe at the beauty of their building.
You will meet me often as you work:
in your companions who share your risk,
in your friends who believe in you enough
to lend their own dreams, their own hands, their own hearts to
your building,
in the people who will find your doorway,
stay awhile and go away knowing that they too can find a
dream.
There will be sun-filled days,
sometimes a little rain, a little variety;
both come from me.
So come now; be content.
It is my dream you dream, my house you build,
my care you witness, my love you share.
And this is the heart of the matter.".'

Brendan Kennelly, *The Heart of the Matter*

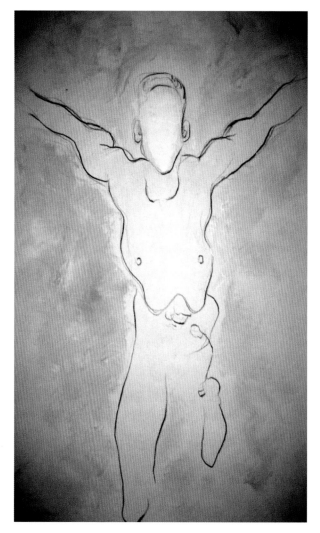

The Cross'

The Road to Emmaus'

Light Bearers

Sunrise

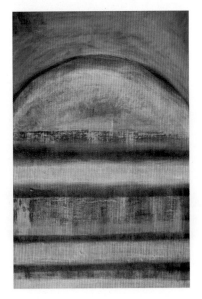

Sunset

Landscape of Life

Landscape of the Soul

Soul

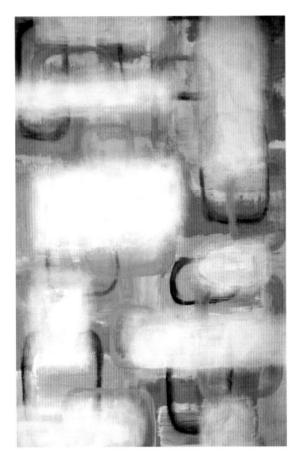

Identity

Passionate Life

Postmodernism

Geometrical

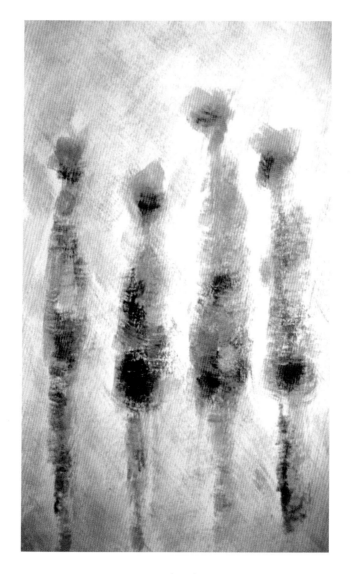

Angels

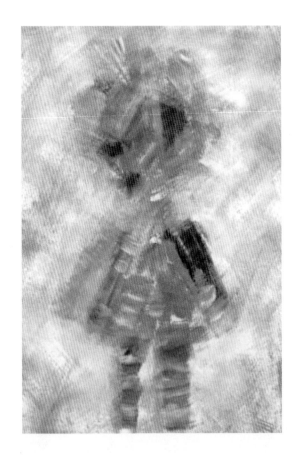

Student

Signpost – STORIES ARE PARABLES FOR LIFE'S JOURNEY

A

'Stories, like dreams, take us in extraordinary directions and, like dreams, they point to hidden messages. The ability to focus our attention on them is indicative of our emotional well being. The universal truths of fairy tales not only show us our place in tradition, but they give us a quiet space to think, a place where crying, gasping and laughing are expected. They encourage our minds to stretch to the new and unknown. They feed our intuition and can be parables for our life's journey.'

Andrew McKenna, 'Swimming Through Dreams'

Ω

The Dream Fixer

'"I'm a dream-fixer", God says. "What I do is take broken dreams and make them into new dreams, slightly different, always better. I can't always re-make the dream just like it was, and I can never undo what was done. But what I do is take broken dreams and use the parts to build a new dream. And the new dream is always better.".'

'Let me give you an example. Remember Joseph and Mary? They were a young couple with a great dream for their marriage, and it became a broken dream. But I sent a messenger in a dream and promised to build a new one. I built a new dream that became the greatest story ever told.'

'There's another example you ought to think about, but I'll let the person tell it himself.'

'I can tell you about broken dreams', Jesus says. 'My life became one. In those last months everything seemed to go wrong, and it turned into a broken dream . . . and God said to me, "I'm a dream-fixer". God said that to me in the garden, when I was desperately trying to save my dream and saw it slipping away. God said, "Don't worry . . . hand it all over to me and I'll see that it becomes a new dream."'

'I thought my death was going to break my dream in half. But my death broke it open, and my dream became a new dream that was beyond anything anyone could have imagined.'

'So it is that we are indeed God's dream. Our dreams don't always last . . . and our dreams are often limited. But God's dream endures, for God can always make new dreams from broken ones. And there is a wideness to God's dream that goes far beyond our narrow horizons. *And God's dream never fails.*'

'The dreamer has a dream for you!'

Taken from Retreat Notes provided by Father Jim Hanley SJ

Signpost—STUDENTS CATCH DREAMS FROM THEIR TEACHERS

A

We may never know when a student catches a dream from us!

A story which illustrates the power of a teacher's influence is the tale told by Brian Cavanaugh:

> In ancient times, a king decided to find and honour the greatest person among his subjects. A man of wealth and property was singled out. Another was praised for her healing powers, another for his business acumen. Many other successful people were brought to the palace, and it became evident that the task of choosing the greatest from among them would be difficult. Finally, the last candidate stood before the king. It was a woman. Her hair was white. Her eyes alone shone with the light of knowledge, understanding and love.
>
> 'Who is this?' asked the king. 'What has she done?'
>
> 'You have seen and heard all the others,' said the King's aide. 'This is their teacher'
>
> The people applauded and the king came down from his throne to crown and honour her.

Anonymous
in Brian Cavanaugh TOR, *The Sower's Seeds* (Mahwa,
NJ: Paulist Press, 1990), 79

Ω

'You take the pen,
and the lines dance.
You take the flute,
and the notes shimmer.
You take the brush,
and the colours sing.
So all things have meaning and beauty
in that space beyond time where you are.
How, then, can I hold anything from you?'

Dag Hammarskjold

Signpost—STUDENTS NEED 'BIG' STORIES, NOT 'THIN' STORIES

A

'It is often said that the end of the twentieth century saw the collapse of the grand master narratives. Fascism, Communism and even, to some extent, Capitalism, gave human beings the road maps to paradise, and crucified millions on the way. In July I visited Auschwitz for the first time. At the entrance there is a big map that shows the railways lines from all over Europe leading to the extermination camp. The lines end at the gas chambers. That is literally the end of the line. Rabbi Hugo Gryn describes how when he arrived at Auschwitz, the entrance to the camp was littered with thrown away condoms and tefillin. I'm not sure what to make of the condoms, but the tefillin were used in Jewish prayer. It was a sign that here in the camp, there was no point in praying any longer. And Auschwitz has become a place of pilgrimage itself, to remind us what happens when we impose road maps on human beings.'

Timothy Radcliffe OP, 'On Christianity in Europe',
Independent Catholic News, 2 May 2005

Ω

'Neil Postman in his book *The End of Education: Redefining the Value of School* talks about "thin" stories and big stories, the latter being those with a transcendent narrative that provides purpose and meaning for our life. "Thin" stories "tend to be stories of economic utility". The story or narrative we are using is "learn how to make a living" but this does not necessarily include the one called "learn how to live". The story of consumerism is "learn how to own as much as possible. Whoever dies with the most toys wins." The goal of such education can be a laptop computer on every desk. I do not think anything is wrong with that, but I do think Postman is correct when he says these stories are not sufficient of themselves; they lack transcendence.'

Rev Tim Costello, 'Ethics in a Competitive Environment', 3 July 1998

Signpost—STORIES AND THE LAYERED CHRISTIAN IMAGINATION

A

'In retrospect, I know this was one moment of many at the time that brought about my inexorable turning towards God and the Catholic faith. This was my introduction to a layered universe, to a conceptual world in which time and space ceased to have the boundaries that my empirically trained mind assumed. Here was a world suffused with a power that did not conform to necessity. Here was a world drenched with grace . . .

A layered reality is part of the Catholic (Christian) imagination. To possess this imagination is to dwell in a universe inhabited by unseen presences—the presence of God, the presence of saints, the presence of one another. There are no isolated individuals but rather unique beings whose deepest life is discovered in and through one another. This life transcends the confines of space and time.'

Wendy Wright, *Sacred Heart, Gateway to God* (New York and London: Orbis and DLT, 2004)

Ω

'A saint might say: "Meditate and pray long enough and you will open yourself up to the other world!" A poet might say: "Stare at a rose long enough and you'll see that there's more there than meets the eye!" A romantic might say: "Just fall in love real deeply or let your heart get broken and you'll soon know there's more to reality than can be empirically measured."

And the mystics of old would say: "Just honour fully what you meet each day and you will find it drenched with grace and divinity.".'

Ronald Rolheiser, 'The Mystical Imagination', 8 May 2005

Signpost—STORIES AND THE NEED TO RETELL THEM

A

GRACE

'Living is dailiness, a simple bread
that's worth the eating. But I have known a wine,
a drunkenness that can't be spoken or sung
without betraying it. Far past Yours or Mine,
even past Ours, it has nothing at all to say;
it slants a sudden laser through common day.

It seems to have nothing to do with things at all,
requires another element or dimension.
Not contemplation brings it; it merely happens,
past expectation and beyond intention;
takes over the depth of flesh, the inward eye,
is there, then vanishes. Does not live or die,
because it occurs beyond the here and now,
positives, negatives, what we hope and are.
Not even being in love, or making love,
brings it. It plunges a sword from a dark star.

Maybe there was once a word for it. Call it grace.
I have seen it, once or twice, through a human face.'

Judith Wright
in *Collected Poems 1942-85* (Sydney: Angus and Robertson,
1994), 331-332

Ω

'Our time is short. People will come after us, and they will tell the stories again. In Aboriginal society that is how we survived— telling the stories, sharing the knowledge, showing the places to gather food and water, passing on the ceremonies. As we grow older, we continue to pass on the stories to our children in our communities. Through our words and actions we tell them about our ways. We let them see beyond the negative images through which our people are often portrayed. We help them grow strong to make their judgments. The words describing these twelve circles pass on the story, as did the twelve Apostles. Without them, we wouldn't have heard about Jesus' life. Like the apostles, we are called to pass on the Good News of Jesus. It is a repeating story—about life, growth and telling the story to others. We believe it is always God's time.'

Miriam-Rose Ungunmerr Baumann, *The Spirit of the Lord is Upon Me* (Melbourne: Jesuit Publications, 2005), 13

Signpost—THE POWER OF TEACHERS' OWN STORIES

A

'I had a very special teacher in high school many years ago whose husband unexpectedly died suddenly of a heart attack. About a week after his death, she shared some of her insight with a classroom of students.'

'Before class is over, I would like to share with all of you a thought that is unrelated to class, but which I feel is very important. Each of us is put here on earth to learn, share, love, appreciate and give of ourselves. None of us knows when this fantastic experience will end. It can be taken away at any moment. Perhaps this is God's way of telling us that we must make the most out of every single day.

Her eyes beginning to water, she went on, "So I would like you all to make me a promise. From now on, on your way to school, or on your way home, find something beautiful to notice. It doesn't have to be something you see; it could be a scent— perhaps of freshly baked bread wafting out of someone's house, or it could be the sound of the breeze slightly rustling the leaves in the trees, or the way the morning light catches one autumn leaf as it falls gently on the ground. Please look for those things, and cherish them. For, although it may sound trite to some, these things are the stuff of life. The little things we are put here on earth to enjoy. The things we often take for granted. We must make it important to notice them, for at any time . . . it can all be taken away."

The class was completely quiet. We all picked up our books and filed out of the room silently. That afternoon, I noticed more things on my way home from school than I had that whole semester. Every once in a while, I think of that teacher and remember what an impression she made on all of us, and I try to appreciate all of those things that sometimes we all overlook. Take notice of something special you see on your lunch hour today. Go barefoot. Or walk on the beach at sunset. Stop off on the way home tonight to get an ice-cream cone. For as we get older, it is not the things we did that we often regret, but the things we didn't do!'

St Ignatius Parish School, Toowong, Newsletter, 18 November 2005

Ω

'He taught in the Temple every day. The chief priests and the scribes, in company with the leading citizens, tried to do away with him, but they could not find a way to carry this out because the whole people hung on his words.'

Luke 19:47–48

Signpost—THE POWER OF A STUDENT'S STORY

A

THE INCARNATION AND CHRISTMAS
SHARON'S CHRISTMAS PRAYER

'She was five,
sure of the facts,
and recited them
with slow solemnity
convinced every word
was revelation.
She said

they were so poor
they had only peanut butter and jelly sandwiches
to eat
and they went a long way from home
without getting lost. The lady rode
a donkey, the man walked, and the baby
was inside the lady.
They had to stay in a stable
with an ox and an ass (hee-hee)
but the Three Rich Men found them
because a star lited the roof
Shepherds came and you could
Pet the sheep but not feed them.
Then the baby was borned.
And do you know who he was?
Her quarter eyes inflated
to silver dollars.
        The baby was God.
        And she jumped in the air

whirled round, dove into the sofa
and buried her head under the cushion
which is the only proper response
to the Good News of the Incarnation.'

From John Shea, *The Hour of the Unexpected*, quoted in Ronald
Rolheiser, *The Holy Longing* (New York: Doubleday, 1999), 71,
72

'What the Incarnation is saying is that henceforward God is
exactly where we are . . . and only there is He to be found.'

Karl Rahner SJ, quoted in one of Fr Richard Rohr's talks on
the Trinity

Signpost—THE POWER OF A SCHOOL'S STORY

A

'In the year 2000, St Ignatius' College Riverview in Sydney opened a new Senior Boarding House named after one of its most distinguished alumni, Dr Kevin Fagan. Kevin Fagan came to Riverview from Launceston on a Bursary in 1923 and was Dux of the School in both his final two years. He progressed to Sydney University to study Medicine and display his diverse talents as a resident at St John's College. Kevin later returned home to Hobart to practise Medicine and joined the Army as a surgeon when war broke out in 1939. He went to Singapore with the 8th Division and, after being captured by the Japanese, became a prisoner of war in Changi. While others like Sir Weary Dunlop received much publicity, Kevin Fagan was no less a war hero in the way he tended to the Australian and British soldiers on the infamous Burma-Thailand railway. Carrying their gear for them when they were too weary to carry it themselves, skilfully operating on them with the crudest of instruments available to him, Kevin Fagan was an inspiration to the men he served. One author wrote of Dr Kevin Fagan that he was "the most inspiring man I have ever met . . . it was no exaggeration that many people survived this ordeal as a result of his personal efforts . . . some 20,000 British and Australian troops share my view".'

An excerpt from my Homily at the Opening of the Boarding House in August, 2000

A fortnight or so ago I received a letter from one of my long-standing friends, Dr Bill Ryan, of Nowra. He wrote: 'I had the extraordinary privilege of working under the guidance of Kevin Fagan, when a resident at Lewisham Hospital. He treated, among others, many severe burns cases. One such . . . went to sleep with a lighted cigarette and suffered very extreme burns. Dr Fagan grafted the burns and I was with him when he came to change the dressings – he always did the first change himself. He completed the task and departed. When I returned to the patient, he said "Gawd, he's got the touch of an angel—who is he?"'

'The touch of an angel'. Those words seem to sum up beautifully the life of Kevin Fagan both as a Doctor and as a fine human being. His son-in-law, Dr Allan Passmore, sent me some material from the Australian War Museum on Dr Kevin Fagan's care of the Prisoners of War while a prisoner himself for 3 years in that hell hole, the Burma-Thai railway. We have other quotations on display in the foyer of the new building, but here are just two from soldiers for whom he cared as prisoners of war.

'To many an unfortunate digger and others who rolled and tossed and cried out with the well nigh insufferable agony of those . . . ulcers came a man who ceased suffering and pain and taking limbs off in many cases he put them on the road to home again. That man's name is a "bye" (sic) word today, Major Fagan. Young, cool, remarkably clever, with my own eyes I have seen him performing some ghastly operations on rude bamboo operating tables between the bamboo huts which were the wards of Kamburi Hospital. With Japanese guards amongst the interested spectators, I have seen him go to work on some ulcer sufferer with uncanny sureness and with supreme confidence in his own undoubted ability to send that sufferer back to the ward where a little later one would see the smiling face which was before grey with pain.'

Yes, Major Fagan, the diggers' children will hear your name spoken with feelings of gratitude for many a long day to come. For the noble work you did, your name will be memorable.

And another soldier had this to say: 'He not only did a

wonderful job for me, but also for hundreds of men. What is more, on one occasion while I was still on my back, he brought me two eggs, and just prior to his departure for Tamarkan, he gave me five eggs, which under the circumstances were gifts much more acceptable and infinitely more precious than all the tea in China . . . '

Ω

'For I was hungry and you gave me food, I was thirsty and you gave me drink, I was a stranger and you made me welcome, lacking clothes and you clothed me, sick and you visited me, in prison and you came to see me.'

Matthew 25:35–36

Signpost—THE POWER OF ANOTHER SCHOOL'S STORY

A

'In 1995 I read the amazing adventure of two young men—Ray Parer (alumnus of my old school, Xavier College, in Melbourne) and John McIntosh—who flew their battered bi-plane from Britain to Australia in 1920. It was the first single engine aircraft to make the journey which lasted 208 days.'

Rowan Ayers wrote in *Good Weekend,* July 29 1995:

'The journey to Darwin took six months and 25 days. It was a remarkable saga of foolhardiness, courage, humour, drama, excitement, frustration and endurance. They crashed and forced-landed many times, often doing serious damage; but somehow they managed to repair their rackety bi-plane and get it back in the air.'

Ω

In 1985 this very fine reflection on the power of the imagination appeared in the August 10 edition of *The Age.* I understand it was written by Sir James Darling, Headmaster of Geelong Grammar School from 1930 to 1961, and a highly significant figure in the development of Australian education.

'The Victorian Government and the Melbourne City Council are stirring their citizens' imaginations with visions of city developments. They are considering proposals to raise a skyscraper above the Museum station; build a spectacular complex of edifices on the Yarra's south bank; restructure the

Regent Theatre, involving alterations to the City Square; erect a national tennis centre on Flinders Park. Now comes a vision of Melbourne as a city not just on a river, but on the bay—with palm-lined boulevards linking the business centre and the beaches and revamped piers with tourist attractions at Port Melbourne. All the schemes have been described as "imaginative".

Creative activity begins not simply by thinking about it, but by imagining it. All planning, whether of a city, a space probe, a gadget for separating egg whites from yolks, or an epic poem, begins with a picture in someone's mind's eye.

As a case in point, Milton wrote *Paradise Lost* just after a new Copernican system had come in. With his intellect the poet believed the new concepts, but they had not yet seized his imagination. Accordingly, it was his mental picture of the old Ptolemaic astronomy—a stationary Earth and the sun revolving around it—that set the scenario for his great epic . . .

The way we habitually imagine ourselves, our fellow men and what we call God is one of the most formative factors in life. Let anyone picture in his or her imagination the kind of person they long to be, and view that picture frequently and steadily enough, and they will be drawn towards it. Within the imagination resides much of the power to control our health, achieve our goals and develop our characters.

Christ knew the power of a fired imagination to motivate people. He enrolled as learners a group of individuals whose horizons were bounded by a country lake. He led them to visualise themselves as the salt of the earth and the light of the world. He filled their imaginations with pictures of themselves carrying his message to "the uttermost parts of the Earth".

As they caught that vision, their backs straightened and a new gleam came into their eyes. They set out to turn that mental picture into a reality—and changed history.'

Teaching and Freeing

PREVIEW WINDOW

Teachers are liberators and healers by nature of the very work they perform on a daily basis. One of the principal goals of their ministry is for their students to become people who can live their lives at depth, a depth where superficial changes do not disturb them. Their teaching is training young men and women to be truly free, to stand against unthinking slavery of any form—habits that change, changing opinions, idols of clay or congratulation. Many of the following reflections focus, therefore, on the *truth* and the need to help young people keep searching for it all their lives—free from fear, prejudice and false assumptions of any kind.

Signpost—GOOD TEACHING IS DISPOSING NOT IMPOSING

A

'When they drew near to the village to which they were going, he made as if to go on; but they pressed him to stay with them.'

Luke 24:28

Ω

'As Jesus in this scene leaves the two disciples free—he declines to impose himself on them in any way—so every good teacher leaves his or her students free. The teacher as a liberator offers his students great healing.

"To let go is to allow something or someone to be left behind in such a way that we are free to continue toward new country that is waiting to be revealed to us . . . Letting go is an attitude that grows within us. It is never complete until it is acted upon.".'

Joyce Dupp, *Praying Our Goodbyes* (Indiana: Ave Maria Press, 1988), 101

Signpost—GOOD TEACHING OFFERS SALVATION IN THE HERE AND NOW

A

'It is no accident that the term "salvation" is closely linked to the word "salve", to heal. Salvation and liberation and healing are one of a kind. "Whatever contributes to the well-being of mankind, whatever is good and noble and lovely and true is the experience of salvation. Salvation is not reserved for the future alone. It is present when a family sits down at a family celebration in thanksgiving for the goodness they have received and the goodness they contribute to each other and enjoy fine food and good wine and great company.".'

Brennan Manning, *A Glimpse of Jesus: The Stranger to Self-Hatred* (San Francisco: Harper, 2004),

Ω

'I shall give you a new heart, and put a new spirit in you; I shall remove the heart of stone from your bodies and give you a heart of flesh instead. I shall put my spirit in you, and make you keep my laws and sincerely respect my observances.'

Ezekiel 36:26–27

Signpost—GOOD TEACHING BLENDS
FAMILIARITY WITH DISTANCE

A

'A teacher can do a great deal, a very great deal—dammit, he can change lives—but, however compelling he is, however successful in gaining examination results or in establishing rapport, he must keep his feet on the ground, keep a little detachment and never for one moment imagine he is indispensable. The trick for the teacher, and it's the trickiest aspect of a tricky business, is to be involved in an unobtrusively caring and very professional way, while also taking care to keep a part of himself to himself. That way his pupils learn, and that way they learn to leave: to become independent.'

Jonathan Smith, *The Learning Game: A Teacher's Inspirational Story*
(London: Little Brown, 2000), 117

Ω

'Education is one of the healing professions, and its instruments are the living model and the word. Our tool as teachers is the word. The word is a two-edged sword, able to be used either to bless or to curse. We teachers may use the word to instruct or to mislead, and we may use the word to create or to destroy. A teacher can stand before a child, a young life, and bless, instruct and create or he can curse, mislead or destroy. The teacher has enormous power and responsibility in his or her hands. The good teacher is an enabler—he or she who enables the pupils in front of them and thereby empowers them to earn their place. The teacher is he or she who frees, who frees from ignorance and thus allows the child to be released for the energies of the mind and the imagination, without the exercise of which none would ever be fully alive or fully human.'

Greg O'Kelly SJ, 'Why Teach?' A Rostrum speech given on 6 March 1992

Signpost—GOOD TEACHERS ARE TRANSPARENT TO THE WORLD

A

'Teachers accomplish their task best when they are transparent to the world.'

'A spirituality developed in the context of a teaching life would have to strive to maintain an ongoing openness toward new and diverse ways of letting people learn, but especially toward letting oneself learn how to let others learn . . . so that in "seeing" the teacher they would learn the taught.'

Ignacio L Gotz, 'Spirituality and Teaching'

Ω

There are 5 pitfalls or sins for Teachers who are not free:

◆ Partiality and fanaticism
◆Capitulation to mediocrity
◆Self-assurance to the point of dogmatism
◆ Allowing flashy technology to supplant mystery
◆ The demise of questioning brought about by the subordination of the mind to power, of the teacher to the administrator, of truth to political correctness, of invention to repetition

Ignacio L Gotz, as above

Signpost—TEACHERS LIBERATE STUDENTS IN SHARING THEIR COMMITMENT TO SEARCH FOR THE TRUTH

A

'If you make my word your home
you will indeed be my disciples,
you will learn the truth
and the truth will make you free.'

John 8:32

Ω

'About fifteen years ago, a young man, still in his twenties,
produced an award-winning movie, "Sex, Lies and
Videotapes". The story is rather simplistic and crass at times,
but overall teaches a lesson that could be from John's Gospel:
The hero of the story, a young man with a bad history in the
area of sexuality, resolves to make himself better by making a
vow to never again tell a lie, even a small one.
Like the man who's born blind in John's Gospel, that vow
brings him to health. He gets better, much better. He then sets
up a video camera and invites people to come and tell their
stories. Those who tell the truth also get better, healthier, and
those who lie and hide their infidelities continue to deteriorate
in both health and happiness. The truth does set us free.'

Ronald Rolheiser, 'Lies Warp the Soul Like a Board in the
Rain', in *The Western Catholic Reporter*, 18 July 2005

Signpost—KEEPING CLOSE TO THE TRUTH IS GOOD FOR THE SOUL AND KEEPS US CLOSE TO GOD

A

'A friend of mine, an alcoholic in recovery, is fond of saying: "Alcoholism is only 10 per cent about a chemical, and 90 per cent about dishonesty. You can drink, as long as you do so honestly." He draws a wider moral axiom from this, adding: "In fact, you can do anything, as long as don't have to lie about it! It's dishonesty, living a double life, that kills the soul and kills families.".'

Ronald Rolheiser, 'Lies Warp the Soul Like a Board in the Rain', in *The Western Catholic Reporter*, 18 July 2005

Ω

'He who is of the truth hears my voice.'
John 18:38

Signpost—GOOD TEACHERS FREE THEIR STUDENTS BY DEMONSTRATING THAT TRUTH AND POPULAR SUPPORT ARE NOT NECESSARILY THE SAME THING

A

We want students who can distinguish between truth and consensus.

'Whilst the digital age has dramatically increased the volume of information we are exposed to, there is no reason to think that it has added anything to our capacity to seek truth or face reality. In fact there are good reasons for thinking that it has done the opposite. I can lose myself in information, choose what I want to know, put a spin on what I want others to hear and move further and further away from truth or reality, without even noticing. That scene from the movie "A Few Good Men" stands out in my mind, where Jack Nicholson delivers that wonderful line to the two sincere army officers: "You want the truth? You can't handle the truth.".'

Felicity McCutcheon, 'Truth in the Bible'. A paper delivered at the DAN (*Dialogue Australasia Network*) Colloquium, Adelaide, 15 April, 2004

Ω

'I can charge you in the presence of God and of Jesus Christ who is to judge the living and the dead, and by His appearing and His kingdom: preach the word, be urgent in season and out of season, convince, rebuke, and exhort, be unfailing in patience and in teaching. For the time is coming when people will not endure sound teaching, but having itchy ears will accumulate for themselves teachers to suit their own likings, and will turn away from listening to the truth and wander into myths.'

2 Timothy 1:1–4

Signpost—GOOD TEACHING ENABLES STUDENTS TO BE READY AND OPEN TO SEE THE TRUTH

A

'One source of our crisis of truth is that our lives are so hectic and frenetic that we do not have the time to see each other or anything properly. Our preoccupation for truth, for accountability, means that we have to spend so much time filling in forms, making reports, compiling statistics, that we have no time to open our eyes and see. When Wittgenstein was asked how philosophers should greet each other, he replied "take your time". So a spirituality of truth would invite us to slow down, be quiet, and let our hearts and minds be stretched open. Simone Weil writes that we "do not obtain the most precious gifts by going in search of them but by waiting for them . . . This way of looking is, in the first place, attentive. The soul empties itself of all its own contents in order to receive the human being it is looking at, just as he is, in all his truth.".'

Timothy Radcliffe OP, 'The Crisis of Truth Telling in Our Society', The 19th Eric Symes Abbott Memorial Lecture 2004

Ω

'Jesus made a tour through all the towns and villages, teaching . . . proclaiming the good news and healing.'

Matthew 9:35

Signpost—GOOD TEACHING HELPS STUDENTS TO SEE THAT STEREOTYPING PEOPLE CANNOT CONTAIN SOMETHING AS LARGE AS THE TRUTH

A

'God is magnetized by the truth, and there you will find him, like the linnet dipping in the stream.'

Mark Helprin in *How Can I Find God?*, edited by James Martin (Missouri: Ligouri, 1997), 64

Ω

'It is dangerous and counterproductive, at least in the area of faith, theology, and preaching, to self-define . . . Both liberals and conservatives carry important truths and defend values that must, in the name of God and truth, be defended. But those truths and values are generally too encrusted within liberal or conservative ideology to be palatable to anyone of the opposite persuasion.

For example, if I present myself as a liberal, a feminist, an ecologist, a gay-rights activist, or as a social justice advocate, roughly half of the population everywhere will already be defensive and suspicious of my truth, motives, and agenda, long before I get to speak a word.

The same is true if I present myself as a conservative, a traditionalist, an advocate for conservative values, or as someone who, above all else, is concerned with proper doctrine, boundaries, safety, and order.

Roughly half the population everywhere will conclude that I have nothing of value to say to them, long before I've even had a chance to speak. Why?

Because, in both cases, whether I present myself as a liberal or a conservative, the general experience has been that because of this self-definition, I will be selective in my sympathies, intolerant of those who think differently, incapable of genuinely appreciating what the other side has to say, and that I will use authority or intellectual intimidation to shut down debate and will be mean-spirited towards those whom I perceive as less enlightened or less orthodox than I.'

Ronald Rolheiser, 'Speaking Our Truth from a Deeper Place', 23 October 2005
Can be found on Ronald Rolheiser webpage in Column Archive

Signpost—GOOD TEACHING HELPS STUDENTS TO SEE THAT THE TRUTH IS FAR MORE THAN A LIST OF FACTS

Ω

'Truthfulness, then, is not just the reporting of facts. Alasdair MacIntyre maintains that facts, like gentlemen's wigs and telescopes, were not invented until the seventeenth century. Truth is the basis of human community. It is the medium in which we encounter and belong to each other. St Augustine talked of humanity as "the community of truth" . . . To lie was not just to fail to be accurate. It is destructive of language, the basis of human solidarity . . . For us, there might not appear to be much of a difference between a true remark that misleads and a lie. That is because we do not have that profound sense of the sacredness of true words as the foundation of human belonging. Lies pollute our natural environment. We die spiritually, like fish in a polluted river.'

Timothy Radcliffe OP, 'The Crisis of Truth Telling in Our Society', *op cit*

Ω

'These are the very things that God has revealed to us through the Spirit for the Spirit reaches the depths of everything, even the depths of God. After all, the depths of a man can only be known by his own spirit, not by any other man, and in the same way the depths of God can only be known by the Spirit of God. Now instead of the spirit of the world we have received the Spirit that comes from God, to teach us to understand the gifts that he has given us. Therefore, we teach, not in the way in which philosophy is taught, but in the way that the Spirit teaches us; we teach spiritual things spiritually.'

1 Corinthians 2:10–13

'Let us pray

God,
You are the supreme teacher
who illuminates human beings with truth.
Make me your echo and allow me to sow
truth and goodness.
Let me be passionate about truth and justice
and warm my heart with your commandments.
Grant me the gift of conveying, teaching, leading
and indicating your ways.
Direct my mind to your truth and my hands to kind acts.
I am small and frail in your light,
but allow me to fulfill my difficult mission.

We ask this thrugh Christ our Lord.
Amen.'

Signpost—GOOD TEACHING HELPS STUDENTS TO SEE THAT LYING CORRUPTS THE SOUL AND TAKES US AWAY FROM GOD

A

'And Jesus read from the scroll of the prophet Isaiah,

"The spirit of the Lord has been given to me,
For he has anointed me.
He has sent me to bring the good news to the poor,
To proclaim liberty to captives
And to the blind new sight,
To set the downtrodden free,
To proclaim the Lord's year of favour.".'

Luke 4:18–19

Ω

'People often say that the Church is hung up on sex. For most of the Christian tradition the Church has been far more preoccupied with lying. In Dante's *Inferno* the top circles of Hell, where people get off lightest, are reserved for people who got carried away by their passions. They desired the good, but got themselves into a mess by desiring it wrongly. The middle regions of Hell were reserved for people who desired what was bad, above all for the violent. But the absolute pits were kept for those who undermined human community: the liars, the fraudulent, the flatterers, the forgers, and worst of all the traitors. Sometimes the modern Church does get a bit hung up about sex, and this suits the media, since it locks the gospel into a safe little box where it can be mocked. But for a traditional

Christian, lying is seen as much more serious. Which you may or may not consider a consolation!'

Timothy Radcliffe OP, 'The Crisis of Truth Telling in Our Society', *op cit*

'The art of schoolmastering, the art of education, was to make that young person realize that he had a talent which I, as an adult, hadn't got. That was the basis of my respect for that person and also gave that person, that young life, a sense of his worth. I could never be a teacher without being a learner— and leaders must always be learners.'

Cardinal Basil Hume, *In My Own Words* (London: Hodder & Stoughton, 1999), 83

Signpost—AS CAREFUL WORDSMITHS, GOOD TEACHERS HELP STUDENTS TO UNDERSTAND THE LIFE-GIVING POWER OF WORDS

A

'A spirituality of truthfulness includes a profound sense of the power of the words that we use to heal or harm. All day long we exchange words: gossiping, telling the news, joking, even giving boring lectures. Truthfulness requires not just that the words are accurate, factual, but that they are constructive, giving life and not death dealing . . . There is construction and annihilation. Parents and children, men and women, when facing each other in exchange of speech, are at ultimate risk. One word can cripple a human relation, can do dirt on hope. The knives of saying cut deepest.'

Timothy Radcliffe OP, 'The Crisis of Truth Telling in Our Society', *op cit*

Ω

'And to some his gift was that they should be apostles; to some prophets; to some, evangelists; to some pastors and teachers; so that the saints together make a unity in the work of service, building up the body of Christ.'

Ephesians 4:11–12

Signpost—GRATITUDE KEEPS US CLOSE TO THE LIBERATING POWER OF THE TRUTH

A

'To ask God for what I desire and to thank God when I receive it is merely to live in the real world. It is to open our eyes to the pure gratuity of being. The word "thank" derives from "think". Thanking is thinking truly . . . We are not ultimately producers and consumers but the recipients of gifts. I have often been struck in Muslim countries by the call of the muezzin to prayer, reminding one of the Creator of all good things.'

Timothy Radcliffe OP, 'The Crisis of Truth Telling in Our Society', *op cit*

Ω

'The Word became flesh,
he lived among us, and we saw His glory,
the glory that he has from the Father
as only Son of the Father,
full of grace and truth . . .

Indeed, from his fullness
we have, all of us, received –
one gift replacing another,
for the Law was given through Moses,
grace and truth have come
through Jesus Christ.'

John 1:14,16–17

Signpost—GOOD TEACHING WILL SHOW THAT THE REAL TRUTH OF A PERSON IS MUCH BIGGER THAN WHAT IS VISIBLE TO THE EYE

A

'We are God's work of art, created in Christ Jesus to live the good life as from the beginning he had meant us to live it.'

Ephesians 2:10

Ω

'So if I am to describe a human being truthfully, it is not enough for me just to describe what is before my eyes. I am reaching out for what cannot be fully told now, what can only be glimpsed at the edge of language. Truthfulness drives us often to poetry and . . . Seamus Heaney writes of poetry as giving us an intimation of "that more radiant and generous life which the imagination desires".'

Timothy Radcliffe OP, 'The Crisis of Truth Telling in Our Society', *op cit*

Signpost—GOOD TEACHING WILL SHOW THAT THE TRUTH WILL ALWAYS TRIUMPH

A

'When I despair, I remember that all through history, the way of truth and love has always won. There have been murderers and tyrants, and for a time they seem invincible. But in the end they always fall. Think of it, always.'

Ghandi

Ω

'Just as each of our bodies has several parts and each part has a separate function, so all of us, in union with Christ, form one body, and as parts of it we belong to each other. Our gifts differ according to the grace given us. If your gift is prophecy, then use it as your faith suggests; if administration, then use it for administration; if teaching, then use it for teaching.'

Romans 12:4–7

Signpost—GOOD TEACHING WILL SHOW THAT THE TRUTH WILL ALWAYS TRIUMPH, THAT THE USE OF FORCE ALWAYS MARKS A FAILURE OF SOME KIND

A

'Good and truth will always triumph, but this triumph must be waited for, not because God wants us to endure pain as some kind of test, but because God, unlike ourselves, doesn't use coercion or violence to achieve an aim. God uses only love, truth, beauty, and goodness and God uses these by embedding them into the universe itself, like a giant moral immune system that eventually, always, brings the body back to health.'

Ron Rolheiser OMI, 'The Way of Truth and Love Has Always Won' in *The Western Catholic Reporter*, 26 April 2004

Ω

'So Pilate went back into the Praetorium and called Jesus to him, "Are you the king of the Jews" he asked. Jesus replied, "Do you ask this of your own accord, or have others spoken to you about me?" Pilate answered, "Am I a Jew? It is your own people and the chief priests who have handed you over to me: what have you done?" Jesus replied: "Mine is not a kingdom of this world; if my kingdom were of this world, my men would have fought to prevent my being surrendered to the Jews. But my kingdom is not of this kind." "So you are a king then?" said Pilate. "It is you who say it" answered Jesus. "Yes, I am a king. I was born for this, I came into the world for this: to bear witness to the truth; and all who are on the side of truth listen to my voice." "Truth?"

said Pilate, "What is that?"; and with that he went out again to the Jews and said, "I find no case against him.".'

John 18:33–38

'God cannot count. Everybody is number one.
God became man not for a crowd but for each one of us.'

Cardinal Basis Hume, *In My Own Words, op cit*, 7

Signpost—TEACHERS FREE PEOPLE WHEN THEY GIVE THEM HOPE

A

'If it were not for our hope, our hearts would break.' (Old Proverb) Teachers are healers when they bring hope to young people.

'Education gives a window through which to imagine a possible future. Once, after beating through thick scrub in northern Uganda to find a group of Sudanese refugees who spent weeks trekking to the border seeking safety, all the people asked of me was for a blackboard and chalk. In the Cambodian camps, which were highly politicised hothouses, I remember the relief of the students of mathematics, who could stretch their minds on a topic that is very difficult to politicise.'

Mark Raper SJ, 'What is a Greater Work?' Occasional Address for the Educational Faculty Graduation Ceremony, Australian Catholic University, Sydney, 23 May 2003

Ω

'God loves each one of us as if there were only one of us.'

St Augustine

Signpost—TEACHERS ALWAYS TEACH THEMSELVES FIRST

A

'Pope John Paul once told an audience of Christians that they might be the only gospel that many people would read that day. All of us are teachers and witnesses, and the teacher always teaches himself or herself first. Leonardo da Vinci's perspective on this was that "The painter always paints himself" and this was picked up by Cardinal Basil Hume when he wrote: "Some people say that in the artist's work you will see something of the artist . . . If you look at a work of art you will always see something of the artist. Some people can recognize composers: that is Mozart, for example, or that is Beethoven. We leave part of ourselves in what we create.".'
(Quoted in Cardinal Basil Hume, *In My Own Words* (London: Hodder & Stoughton, 1999), 30

Ω

'I gave you life, but I cannot live for you,
I can teach you things, but I cannot make you learn.
I can give you direction, but I cannot be there to lead you.
I can allow you freedom, but I cannot account for it.
I can take you to church, but I cannot make you believe.
I can teach you right from wrong, but I cannot decide for you.
I can buy you a beautiful garment, but I can't make you
beautiful inside.
I can offer advice, but I cannot accept it for you.
I can give you love, but I cannot force it upon you.
I can teach you to share, but I cannot make you unselfish.

I can advise you about friends, but I cannot choose them for
you.
I can advise you about sex, but I cannot keep you pure.
I can tell you the facts of life, but I cannot build your
reputation.
I can tell you about drink, but I cannot say "no" for you.
I can tell you about lofty goals, but I cannot achieve them for
you.
I can teach you about kindness, but I cannot force you to be
gracious.
I can warn you about sins, but I cannot make you moral.
I can pray for you, but I cannot make you walk with God.
I can teach you about Jesus, but I cannot make Jesus your
Lord.
I can tell you how to live, but I cannot give you eternal life.'

Anonymous

Signpost—TEACHERS ARE PREPARED TO FACE THEIR FEARS

A

'Lord, help me to remember
that nothing is going to happen to me today
that you and I
together
can't handle.'

Old Preacher's prayer

Ω

'It is eighteen years ago, almost to the day—
A sunny day with the leaves just turning,
The touch-lines new-ruled—since I watched you play
Your first game of football, then, like a satellite
Wrenched from its orbit, go drifting away

Behind a scatter of boys. I can see
You walking away from me towards the school
With the pathos of a half-fledged thing set free
Into a wilderness, the gait of one
Who finds no path where the path should be.

That hesitant figure, eddying away
Like a winged seed loosened from its parent stem,
Has something I never quite grasp to convey
About nature's give-and-take—the small, the scorching
Ordeals which fire one's irresolute clay.
I have had worse partings, but none that so

Gnaws at my mind still. Perhaps it is roughly
Saying what God alone could perfectly show –
How selfhood begins with a walking away,
And love is proved in the letting go.'

C Day Lewis, 1904–1972

Signpost—TEACHERS CAN FREE IF THEY THEMSELVES ARE FREE

A

Teachers as healers, as liberators, seek to free their students from fears, prejudices, false assumptions, and resentments. The teacher can liberate, can heal, only if he or she is free. The teacher can be free only if he or she recognises and acknowledges these challenges in himself or herself.

Ω

'I will just add that a great source of pride in our school is the relationship we have established with the boys. This is indeed something precious and we have got it right: we learned it from those who went before us. They established a wonderful relationship and a balance which we have inherited. But it is something we need to watch, protect, and treasure. We have to strike a happy balance—be on our guard against over-familiarity, becoming "one of the boys", thus winning a spurious success. A certain detachment, a certain self-control, a capacity to say "No" to oneself yet retain warmth and friendship—here is to be found the key to so much we can do for the boys. But ours is a precious tradition which could easily go wrong.'

Cardinal Basil Hume OSB, in *Searching for God* (London: Hodder and Stoughton, 1977)—a series of conferences he gave between 1963 and 1976 to the monastic community at Ampleforth when he was the Abbot.

Signpost—TEACHERS MUST BE BEARERS OF HOPE

A

It was Napoleon, curiously, who said once that 'a leader is a dealer in hope'. Teachers as healers must be bearers of hope for those in their care.

Ω

Youth suicide has been one of the tragic manifestations of the fact that hope is so precious and often so difficult to attain for our young people. The following is an excerpt from my Homily at the funeral Mass for Edwina in February, 2005. I have her parents' permission to publish this:

'In talking with Ian and Karen last Thursday, one of the first things they mentioned to me was their faith in young people, how the young people they know care for one another and look out for one another—both shining qualities in Edwina's all too brief life with us. Her love for her friends, her connection with them, reminded me of the story of the great Italian writer of opera, Puccini, who composed such classic operas as "Madame Butterfly" and "La Boheme". It seems that when he was young he attracted cancer, and he decided to spend his last days writing his final opera, "Turandot", which was one of his most polished pieces. When his friends and disciples would say to him: "You are sick, take it easy and rest", he would always respond, "I'm going to do as much as I can on my great masterwork and it's up to you, my friends, to finish it if I don't." Puccini, however, died before the opera was completed.

Now his friends had a choice. They could forever mourn their friend and return to life as usual—or they could build on his melody and compete what he started. They chose the latter. And so in 1926, at the famous La Scala Opera House in Milan, Italy, Puccini's opera was played for the first time, conducted by the famous conductor, Toscanini. And when it came to the part in the opera where the master had stopped because he died, Toscanini stopped everything, turned around with eyes welling up with tears, and said to the large audience, "This is where the master ends." And he wept. But then, after a few moments, he lifted up his head, smiled broadly, and said, "And this is where his friends began". And he finished the opera.

To the many young people here today, I am sure you can see the point of the story. What response will you make to Edwina's death? What are you going to do about her unfinished masterpiece? I am sure you will want to build on her many gifts and talents outlined for us earlier by Ian and Justin. I would suggest that the most fitting response to the pain of Edwina's death is *life, your life, your* life that is lived better; *your* life lived more generously, *your* life that makes a difference, *your* life that is honest and decent, *your* life that makes beautiful music for Edwina and the Lord. The music does not have to stop here today. You have your choice.'

C Gleeson SJ, Homily, February 2005

Signpost—TEACHERS MUST BE BEARERS OF HOPE TO THEIR STUDENTS

A

'Hope is an echo.'
Carl Sandburg

Ω

'Hope is not a resting-place, but a starting-point. It is a cactus, not a cushion; it should make you jump up and do something. The great Anglo-Irish playwright, George Bernard Shaw, wrote: "Life is no brief candle to me, it is a sort of splendid torch which I've got hold of for the moment and I want to make it burn as bright as possible before handing it on to a future generation. Life for us on earth is brief, although the opportunities are many, and our task is to keep the torch burning brightly so that we can pass it on to those coming behind us. It will not all be easy; there will be pain and hurt. It is worth remembering, however, that on the darkest night the stars shine most brightly. Hope is a periscope which enables us to see over our present problems to future possibilities. While admiring your neighbour's lawn across the fence, do not miss the roses blooming at your feet."

Our readings tonight tell us that hope on its own is only half the story. Someone once said that "when you are worried, give your troubles to God: He will be up all night anyway".'

C Gleeson SJ—an excerpt from a homily to the
Valetants at St Ignatius' College in 1999

Signpost—TEACHERS CAN BE SPARKS OF GOD FOR THEIR STUDENTS

A

'[31]After saying this, what can we add? If God is for us, who can be against us? [32]Since he did not spare his own Son, but gave him up for the sake of all of us, then can we not expect that with him he will freely give us all his gifts? [33]Who can bring any accusation against those that God has chosen? When God grants saving justice [34]who can condemn? *[Is 50:8] Are we not sure that it is Christ Jesus, who died-yes and more, who was raised from the dead and is at God's right hand-and who is adding his plea for us? [35]Can anything cut us off from the love of Christ-can hardships or distress, or persecution, or lack of food and clothing, or threats or violence; [36]as scripture says: For your sake we are being massacred all day long, treated as sheep to be slaughtered? *[Ps 44:22] [37]No; we come through all these things triumphantly victorious, by the power of him who loved us. [38]For I am certain of this: neither death nor life, nor angels, nor principalities, nothing already in existence and nothing still to come, nor any power, [39]nor the heights nor the depths, nor any created thing whatever, will be able to come between us and the love of God, known to us in Christ Jesus our Lord.'

Paul's Letter to the Romans, 8:31–39

Ω

'During the Balkans War I remember reading about Boris Krasovac, a Professor of Music at the Dubrovnik Academy. His family home was utterly destroyed in a firebomb attack and the only thing he had been able to rescue was his violin. He said:

"I've lost everything. I found out that all I really have is me and my life . . . After the attack I had only the clothes I was wearing and my violin. But people—my friends and others I never knew before—came up to me and gave me everything. I was crying, but it was marvellous. I hope after this war is over these sparks of goodness will stay in the people. You can call them the sparks of God . . . We must have hope. Hope dies the last." Hope is the spark of God in us.'

C Gleeson SJ, an excerpt from a Homily at the 1999
Graduation Mass, St Ignatius' College, Riverview

Signpost—TEACHERS BEARING HOPE GIVE STRENGTH TO THOSE WHO ARE TIRING

A

'Did you not know? Had you not heard?
Yahweh is the everlasting God,
he created the remotest parts of the earth.
He does not grow tired or weary,
his understanding is beyond fathoming.
He gives strength to the weary,
he strengthens the powerless.
Youths grow tired and weary,
the young stumble and fall,
but those who hope in Yahweh
will regain their strength,
they will sprout wings like eagles,
though they run
they will not grow weary,
though they walk they will never tire.'

Isaiah 40:28–31

Ω

'Birds sing after a storm.'

This was Rose Kennedy's response to a reporter who asked her how she coped with enduring so much tragedy in her family.

Signpost—TEACHERS BEARING HOPE MAKE MUSIC FOR THEIR STUDENTS

A

'An American friend told me a story of the great violinist, Itzhak Perlman, who suffered from polio as a child and lived most of his life in a wheelchair. On one occasion he was performing a violin concerto when, with an audible ping, one of the strings broke in the first movement. Everyone waited to see what he would do. With astonishing skill, he continued as if nothing had happened, playing through to the finale using only the remaining three strings. The applause, as the concerto ended, was tumultuous, not only for his performance but for his coolness in continuing undaunted. As the noise subsided, he was called on to say a few words to the audience. Sitting in the wheelchair, a living symbol of courage, he spoke just one sentence: "Our job is to make music with what remains.".'

Adapted from an article by Chief Rabbi Jonathan Sacks in *The Times*, September 2002

Ω

'In July 1992, the New York Times told the true story of Vedran Smailovic during the war in Sarajevo. His photograph shows him to be middle-aged, with longish hair and a great bushy moustache. He is dressed in formal evening clothes sitting in a cafe chair in the middle of a street in front of a bakery where mortar fire struck a breadline in late May, killing twenty-two people. He is playing his cello. As a member of the Sarajevo Opera Orchestra, there is little he can do about hate and war— it has been going on in Sarajevo for centuries. Even so, every day for twenty-two days he has braved sniper and artillery fire to play Albinoni's profoundly moving Adagio in G Minor.

Author Robert Fulghum has taken up the running on this larger than life story: "Demagogues lit bonfires of hatred between citizens who belonged to different religions and ethnic groups. Everyone became an enemy of someone else. None was exempt or safe. Men, women, children, babies, grand-parents— old and young—strong and weak—partisan and innocent—all, all were victims in the end. Many were maimed. Many were killed. Those who did not die lived like animals in the ruins of the city.

Except one man. A musician. A cellist. He came to a certain street corner every day. Dressed in formal black evening clothes, sitting in a fire-charred chair, he played his cello. Knowing he might be shot or beaten, still he played. Day after day he came. To play the most beautiful music he knew.

Day after day after day. For twenty-two days.

His music was stronger than hate. His courage stronger than fear. And in time other musicians were captured by his spirit, and they took their places in the street beside him. These acts of courage were contagious. Anyone who could play an instrument or sing found a place at a street intersection somewhere in the city and made music.

In time the fighting stopped.

The music and the city and the people lived on".'

Quoted in Robert Fulghum *Maybe, Maybe Not: Second Thoughts from a Secret Life* (New York: Random House, 1993)

'In the world you will have hardship; but be courageous, I have conquered the world.'

John 16:33

Signpost—TEACHERS BEAR HOPE IN THEIR PREPAREDNESS TO LISTEN

A

'The famous psychotherapist, Viktor Frankl, survived three years in the concentration camps of Dachau and Auschwitz. He once told the story of the woman who phoned him in the middle of the night and calmly told him that she was about to commit suicide. Frankl kept her on the phone and talked her through her depression, giving her reason after reason to carry on living. Eventually she promised him she would not take her life, and she kept her word.

When they met later, Frankl asked her which of the reasons she had found convincing. "None" she replied. What then persuaded her to go on living? Her answer was simple. Frankl had been willing to listen to her in the middle of the night. A world in which someone was prepared to listen to another's distress seemed to her one in which it was worthwhile to live.'

From the Chief Rabbi Jonathan Sacks, an article in *The Times*, December 2002

Ω

'In his book of selected prose, *Finders Keepers*, Irish author Seamus Heaney writes that hope is different from optimism. "It is a state of the soul rather than a response to the evidence. It is not the expectation that things will turn out successfully but the conviction that something is worth working for, however it turns out." There might not have been much optimism amongst the followers of Jesus at 3.00 pm on Good Friday, but there was every reason to hope. Easter is about hope, not optimism.'

From an editorial by C Gleeson SJ on 'Hope, not Optimism' in *Madonna*, March–April 2005

The kind of hope I often think about (especially in hopeless situations) is, I believe, a state of mind, not a state of the world. Either we have hope within us or we don't. Hope is not a prognostication—it's an orientation of the spirit. Each of us must find real, fundamental hope within himself. You can't delegate that to anyone else.

Hope in this deep and powerful sense is not the same as joy when things are going well, or willingness to invest in enterprises that are obviously headed for early success, but rather an ability to work for something to succeed. Hope is definitely not the same thing as optimism. It's not the conviction that something will turn out well, but the certainty that something makes sense, regardless of how it turns out. It is this hope, above all, that gives us strength to live and to continually try new things, even in conditions that seem as hopeless as ours do, here and now. In the face of this absurdity, life is too precious a thing to permit its devaluation by living pointlessly, emptily, without meaning, without love, and finally, without hope.

Vaclac Havel
Disturbing the Peace

Quoted in Gordon Livingstone, *Only Spring: On Mourning the Death of My Son* (Sydney: Hachette Livre, 2000), 192

Signpost—TEACHERS ARE LIGHT BEARERS IN THE DARKNESS WHEN THEY BEAR HOPE

A

'Towards the end of April in 1996 we experienced the horrific massacre of dozens of innocent people at Tasmania's famous tourist spot, Port Arthur. Given its history as a convict prison, there has always been an eerie beauty about this place which witnessed even more death and suffering on that fateful Sunday afternoon. I can remember the young pharmacist, Walter Mikac, whose wife and two daughters were murdered that day, standing up at their funeral service a week later in Melbourne and giving the world the following message of hope: "Do not take your partner for granted, do not take your children for granted. Do not take life for granted. Most importantly, do not take tomorrow for granted. The power of love and creation will always triumph over the power of destruction and revenge".'

From the same *Madonna* editorial by C Gleeson SJ on 'Hope, not Optimism'

Ω

'American author, Ronald Rolheiser OMI, has told the story of how the people of South Africa lived in hope that one day the evils of apartheid would be overcome. To this end they lit candles and placed them in their windows for their neighbours, the government and the whole world, to see their belief. So fearful of this action were the Government that they passed an act to make it illegal to light a candle and place it in a window. In the end, "morally shamed by its own people, the government conceded that apartheid was wrong and dismantled it without a war." Defeated by the hope of the people and brought down by lit candles, apartheid was no more. The light of hope had overcome the darkness once again. The hope of Easter will always shine though.'

Loc cit

Signpost—TEACHERS ARE HEALERS WHEN THEY HELP PEOPLE WALK TALL

A

Teachers are about helping people walk tall—the ministry of healing, in other words.

'We are always both grand and petty . . . The world isn't divided up between big-hearted and small-minded people. Rather our days are divided up between moments when we are big-hearted, generous, hospitable, unafraid, wanting to embrace everyone and those moments when we are petty, over-aware of the unfairness of life, frightened, and seeking only to protect ourselves.

But we are most truly ourselves when what's tall in us takes over and gives back to the world what the short, petty person wrongly takes. John of the Cross, the great mystic, made this insight the centrepiece of his theology of healing. For him, this is the way we heal:

We heal not by confronting all our wounds and selfishness head-on, which would overwhelm us and drown us in discouragement, but by growing to what he calls "our deepest centre". For him, this centre is not first of all some deep place of solitude inside the soul, but rather the furthest place of growth that we can attain, the optimum of our potential.'

Ronald Rolheiser OMI, 'Walking Tall Smothers the Small Talk', in *The Western Catholic Reporter*, week of 17 November 2003

Ω

Zacchaeus 'was anxious to see what kind of man Jesus was, but he was too short and could not see him for the crowd, so he ran ahead and climbed a sycamore tree to catch a glimpse of Jesus who was to pass that way.'

Luke 19:3–4

Jesus the teacher and healer *par excellence* enables Zacchaeus to walk tall in this story.

'Man plans, God laughs'

Yiddish Proverb

Signpost—TEACHERS ARE HEALERS WHEN THEY HELP PEOPLE LOVE THEMSELVES

As love is such an important ingredient in healing, it is worth reflecting on the teacher's capacity to help students love themselves, love others, and love God. 'To love another person is to see the face of God' are those magical words sung towards the end of that exquisite musical, *Les Misérables*.

A

'Love is what's in the room with you at Christmas, if you stop opening presents and listen.' Bobby, age 7

'You really shouldn't say "I love you" unless you mean it. But if you mean it, you should say it a lot. People forget.'
Jessica, age 8

'When my grandmother got arthritis, she couldn't bend over and paint her toenails anymore. So my grandfather does it for her all the time, even when his hands got arthritis too. That's love.' Rebecca, age 8

Ω

'Love is always patient and kind; it is never jealous; love is never boastful or conceited; it is never rude or selfish; it does not take offence, and is not resentful. Love takes no pleasure in other people's sins but delights in the truth; it is always ready to excuse, to trust, to hope, and to endure whatever comes.'

1 Corinthians 13:4–7

Signpost—TEACHERS ARE HEALERS WHEN THEY HELP PEOPLE UNDERSTAND THAT LOVE AND PAIN ARE CONSTANT COMPANIONS

A

'In the Irish Sacred Heart Messenger for July 2004, Maureen MacMahon wrote that "while love is the most beautiful and sought after thing in life, it has its hard edges . . . and painful thorns. To know the love of another is a life-giving experience. To give love is self-enriching. True love makes us free, but it also binds. It commits us to another, even when the petals begin to fade. It is an echo of God's love for us, which is the only perfect love, totally selfless and self-giving."

American author Brian Doyle writes with beautiful humour in his book, "Leaping", about his teaching and preparation of a group of 8 year-olds to receive Holy Communion. He talks to them about the "infinite shapes of love, among them affection and respect". Indeed, he echoes the words of Maureen MacMahon above in showing them that "romance is only a corner of the cloak".

What a wonderful image! If romance is only one corner, and pain and commitment take up another corner, then the joy of intimate friendship must take up the remainder of the cloak and draw us into the folds of God's love. As Thomas Merton would have it, "because we love God is present".'

C Gleeson SJ, editorial in *Madonna*, September–October, 2004

Ω

'Yes, God loved the world so much
that he gave his only Son,
so that everyone who believes in him may not be lost
but may have eternal life.'

John 3:16

Love and fidelity aare mostly a matter of turning up, again and
again, without any expectation of reward. We keep turning up
for life and repeatedly facing what must be faced and helping
others to do the same.

Michael Whelan, 'Reciprocity is Empowering', in *The Mix*, July,
2007, Isssue 114, 1

Signpost—TEACHERS ARE HEALERS WHEN THEY HELP PEOPLE UNDERSTAND THAT TRUE LOVE DOES NOT COME TO AN END

A

'Prior to her impending marriage to Prince Frederik of Denmark in mid-2004, Tasmanian Mary Donaldson spoke of her love for him using the words of the beautiful Sonnet XLIII of Elizabeth Barrett Browning:

> HOW do I love thee? Let me count the ways.
> I love thee to the depth and breadth and height
> My soul can reach, when feeling out of sight
> For the ends of Being and ideal Grace.
> I love thee to the level of everyday's
> Most quiet need, by sun and candle-light.
> I love thee freely, as men strive for Right;
> I love thee purely, as they turn from Praise.
> I love thee with the passion put to use
> In my old griefs, and with my childhood's faith.
> I love thee with a love I seemed to lose
> With my lost saints,—I love thee with the breath,
> Smiles, tears, of all my life!—and, if God choose,
> I shall but love thee better after death.

Not surprisingly, there are echoes of Paul's Letter to the Ephesians here where he prays that we "will, with all the saints, have strength to grasp the breadth and the length, the height and the depth, until knowing the love of Christ, which is beyond all knowledge", we "are filled with the utter fullness of God." (Ephesians 3:18–19) After all, when we want to talk about the extravagant extremes of our love for someone, we immediately think of the love God has for us. "God has more mercy than we have sins to commit", Brian Doyle rightly tells his 8 year-old students in his book "Leaping".'

An excerpt from the editorial in *Madonna*, September–October, 2004

Ω

'I have loved you with an everlasting love, so I am constant in my affection for you.'

Jeremiah 31:3

Signpost—TEACHERS LIBERATE OTHERS WHEN THEY TEACH A CAPACIOUS TRUTH SO DIFFERENT FROM THE MIND-NUMBING OMNISCIENCE OF THE FUNDAMENTALISTS

A

'In almost every society, religion, and culture, people all across the globe seem to be racing eagerly toward the sound bite and headline-clarifying singleness of vision of the fundamentalist. Perhaps this is in reaction to the cacophonous blare of globalization. In the end, they may win the day . . . The truth that sets people free is so capacious that we have to walk around it many times to take in all its facets and dimensions . . . Perhaps Jesus preferred to speak in parables to keep his truth from immediately being set in stone, memorized, or owned. He expected his disciples to have to chew on them a while to unlock their flavor. It was not a lesson we learn easily . . . We contemplate truth as something that can be contained and specified, and yet every formation of it remains incomplete, something we both believe in and live as an open-ended question. As Marilynne Robinson explains, "A question is more spacious than a statement, far better suited to expressing wonder".'

Michael Heher, *The Lost Art of Walking on Water: Reimagining the Priesthood* (Mahwa, NJ: Paulist Press, 2004), 132–134

Ω

'That same day Jesus left the house and sat by the lakeside, but such crowds gathered around him that he got into a boat and sat there. The people all stood on the beach and he told them many things in parables.'

Matthew 13:1–3

Teaching as Blessing

PREVIEW WINDOW

Blessing all manner of persons and things is a very ancient practice in the Christian tradition—a practice not reserved to priests and officials. Teachers are constantly blessing their students—helping them to appreciate what the Irish call a 'thin place', where there is just the thinnest membrane separating the spiritual and material worlds. When Australian cricketer, Matthew Hayden, blesses himself after making a century, he is acknowledging God's partnership with him in achieving this feat. Blessing is about direction-finding, about sourcing, about recognizing that God is the source of everything, that He is not just at the beginning and end of our road but in every step along the way. What richer blessing can teachers offer their students than to uncover for them life's most important values in the journey from God to God?

Signpost—GOOD TEACHING IS ITSELF AN ACT OF BLESSING

A

'Now while he was with them at table, he took the bread and said the blessing; then he broke it and handed it to them. And their eyes were opened and they recognized him; but he had vanished from their sight.'

Luke 24:30–31

Ω

'In the past, the act of blessing has been exercised by people of every rank and class. Parents and teachers blessed their children; rulers blessed their subjects. It is open to everyone to bless, and if we gave more to time to blessing than to brutalizing, we would surely have a more peaceful and appreciative world.

The act of blessing is one that

◆ Affirms
◆ Touches the original goodness in another person
◆ Lets another person know that they are beloved by God.'

From H Nouwen, *Life of the Beloved: Spiritual Living in a Secular World* (New York: Crossroad, 1993), 56–60

Signpost—GOOD TEACHING AND BLESSING ARE ABOUT SOURCING

A

'Blessed be God the Father of our Lord Jesus Christ, who has blessed us with all the spiritual blessings of heaven in Christ. [4]Thus he chose us in Christ before the world was made to be holy and faultless before him in love, [5]marking us out for himself beforehand, to be adopted sons, through Jesus Christ. Such was his purpose and good pleasure, [6]to the praise of the glory of his grace, his free gift to us in the Beloved, [7]in whom, through his blood, we gain our freedom, the forgiveness of our sins. Such is the richness of the grace [8]which he has showered on us in all wisdom and insight. [9]He has let us know the mystery of his purpose, according to his good pleasure which he determined beforehand in Christ, [10]for him to act upon when the times had run their course: that he would bring everything together under Christ, as head, everything in the heavens and everything on earth.'

Ephesians 1:1–10

Ω
To bless is:

◆ to take people back to the true source of all gifts, God
◆ to remind people that they are a blessing, a gift to us

Signpost—GOOD TEACHING AND BLESSING ARE ABOUT SEEING LIFE AS GIFT

A

'There is a story told about an old desert father of the fourth century who was walking along the road with his disciples and they saw a beautiful woman coming along on a donkey in the other direction. And the old man looked at her appreciatively while the disciples fixed their eyes on the ground lest they be led into temptation. A couple of miles later one of the disciples said: "Father, why did you gaze at that lovely woman?" And the old man said, "Oh, so you are still thinking about her, are you? You saw her only as a source of temptation. I saw her as one of the wonders of God's creation". All education is helping people to see things as they are. And that it is to say, it is ultimately learning to see things as created not as a commodity but as a gift.'

Timothy Radcliffe OP, *I Call You Friends* (London: Continuum, 2004), 266–267

Ω

'May the Lord bless you and keep you.
May the Lord let his face shine on you and be gracious to you.
May the lord uncover his face to you and bring you peace.'

Numbers 6:24–26

Signpost—GOOD TEACHING HELPS PEOPLE SEE THEMSELVES AS A BLESSING

A

'We are all a means of blessing for one another. You have to want to be a blessing, of course. And who knows? Maybe the problem is not that we don't see the blessings around us. It may be that we fail to see ourselves as blessings. And so we aren't.'

Joan Chittister OSB, *Listen With the Heart: Sacred Moments in Everyday Life* (London: Sheed and Ward, 2003), 8

Ω

'How rich and deep are the wisdom and the knowledge of God! We cannot reach to the root of his decisions or his ways. *Who has ever known the mind of the Lord? Who has ever been his adviser? Who has ever given anything to him, so that his presents come only as a debt returned?* Everything there is comes from him and is caused by him and exists for him. To him be glory for ever! Amen.'

Romans 11:33–36

Signpost—GOOD TEACHING HELPS PEOPLE SEE THEMSELVES AS A BLESSING RATHER THAN AS A CURSE

A

'The truth is that each of us is necessarily either blessing or curse to the people around us. How much better—both for them and for ourselves—to be a conscious blessing to another than a burden on the way.'

J Chittister OSB, *Listen With the Heart, op cit*, 10

Ω

'On my book shelves I have a book written by an old Dominican called *Les Cicatrices* (*The Scars*). In this book he tells how he came to Christ through the hurts of his life. And when he gave it to me he wrote a dedication saying, "For Timothy, who knows that the scars can become the doors of the sun." Every wound we have can become a door for the rising sun . . . We must face the fact that we too have wounded each other. So often I have seen the brethren wound other members . . . unintentionally, through a patronizing word or by a failure to treat women or lay people as our equals. But it is not only the brothers. We all have the power to hurt; the power to speak words that wound, the power of the priests over the laity, of men over women and of women over men, of religious over laity, of superiors over the members of their community, of the rich over the poor, of the confident over the fearful.'

Timothy Radcliffe OP, *I Call You Friends* (London: Continuum, 2004), 214–215

Signpost—WHEN GOOD TEACHING HELPS PEOPLE SEE THEMSELVES AS BLESSED, THEY HAVE A SOURCE OF STRENGTH FOR WHATEVER LIES AHEAD

A

'The blessings that we give to each other are expressions of the blessing that rests on us for all eternity. It is the deepest affirmation of our true self. It is not enough to be chosen. We also need an ongoing blessing that allows us to hear in an ever-new way that we belong to a loving God who will never leave us alone, but will remind us that we are guided by love on every step of our lives . . . "You are my Beloved Son, on you my favor rests". This was a blessing, and it was that blessing that sustained Jesus through all the praise and blame, admiration and condemnation that followed.'

Henri Nouwen, *Life of the Beloved: Spiritual Living in a Secular World* (New York: Crossroad, 1993), 59–60

Ω

'For the heavens are as high above earth as my ways are above your ways, my thoughts above your thoughts. For, as the rain and the snow come down from the sky and do not return before having watered the earth, fertilizing it and making it germinate to provide seed for the sower and food to eat, so it is with the word that goes from my mouth: it will not return to me unfulfilled or before having carried out my good pleasure and having achieved what it was sent to do.'

Isaiah 55: 9–11

Signpost—GOOD TEACHING AND BLESSING SHOW THAT ALL IS 'ON LOAN' TO US

A

'Oh only for short a while you
have loaned us to each other,
because we take form in your act
of drawing us,
And we take life in your painting us,
and we breathe in your singing us.
But only for so short a while
have you loaned us to each other.'

Ancient Aztec Indian prayer, source unknown

'This "on loan" philosophy is the first and most important
attitude of a pilgrim heart . . . When we look upon all life as
being on loan to us, we look at it differently. We look at this
loan for what it is—purely gift, given to us out of love. We
reverence all that we have and take great joy in it, but we do
not grasp, cling to, or hoard our treasures . . .'

Joyce Rupp, *Praying Our Goodbyes* (Indiana: Ave Maria Press,
1988), 69, 71

Ω

'Listen, heavens, while I speak:
hear, earth, the words that I shall say!
May my teaching fall like the rain,
may my word drop down like the dew,

like showers on the grass,
like light rain on the turf!
For I shall proclaim the name of Yahweh.
Oh, tell the greatness of our God!'
Deuteronomy 32:1–3

Signpost—GOOD TEACHING AND BLESSING EMPOWER PEOPLE

A

'One day
I would like
to teach,
just a few people,
many and beautiful things,
that would
help them when
they will
one day teach—
a few people.'

A Teacher's Prayer

Ω

'It was at this time that Jesus came from Nazareth in Galilee and was baptized in the Jordan by John. And at once, as he was coming up out of the water, he saw the heavens torn apart and the Spirit, like a dove, descending on him. And a voice came from heaven, "You are my Son, the Beloved; my favor rests on you".'

Mark 1:9–11

Signpost—GOOD TEACHING AND BLESSING AND THE POWER OF NAMING

As children we used to chant the words: 'Sticks and stones will break my bones, but names will never hurt me.' I have never really believed this message, and the older I get, the more convinced I have become that names can hurt and do permanent damage. Naming people and things is an act of blessing, and teachers are often in the position of providing names that build up or names that tear down.'

A

'We give life to everything, in other words, by naming it. We make relationships even with things that are not present, are not human, by naming them. We invest life with meaning by naming the things around us that give us identity, direction and character. It is a tradition as old as the Old Testament itself . . . Naming is clearly a holy act, an act of creation. It begets identity. But it can also destroy relationships. It's a powerful device that deserves to be used with caution, with reverence, with sacred trust.'

Joan Chittister OSB, *Listen With the Heart, Sacred Moments in Everyday Life* (London: Sheed and Ward, 2003), 44

'What we don't name we enable.'

Joan Chittister OSB, *Called to Question: A Spiritual Memoir* (London: Sheed and Ward, 2004), 133

Ω

'Do not be afraid, for I have redeemed you;
I have called you by your name,
you are mine.
Should you pass through the waters,
I shall be with you;
or through rivers,
they will not swallow you up.
Should you walk through fire,
you will not suffer,
And the flame will not burn you.'

Isaiah 43:1–2

Signpost—GOOD TEACHING AND BLESSING AND THE POWER OF NAMING—FOR GOOD OR EVIL

When I was in primary school, a companion of mine developed a nasty skin disease which prompted his peers to name him 'lepo' (short for 'leprosy'). So destructive of self-esteem was this name that his sickness worsened and his parents were forced to take him away from the school. Fifty years on, I can still feel revulsion at this name and my own inertia in preventing others from using it.

A

'Naming is as much a curse as it is an act of creation. It yields blows from which a person may never recover. Martina Navratilova put it this way: "I came to live in a country I love; some people label me a defector. I have loved men and women in my life; I've been labeled 'the bisexual defector' in print. Want to know another secret? I'm even ambidexterous. I don't like labels. Just call me Martina".'

Joan Chittister OSB, *Listen With the Heart, op cit*, 48

Ω

'Can a woman forget her baby at the breast, feel no pity for the child she has borne? Even if these were to forget, I shall not forget you. Look, I have engraved you on the palms of my hands.'

Isaiah 49:15–16

Signpost—GOOD TEACHERS UTILISE THE POWER OF BLESSING WHEN THEY TEACH RIGHT VALUES

Every time we are blessed we are taken back to the source of all life—our God, who is not just the beginning and end of our journey, but a companion for us in every step along the way. The teaching of right values is a rich blessing for teachers to offer their students.

A

'Values "are the beacons that guide our way through change . . . Values have permanence when not much else sticks around. They are what we hold on to when everything else is throwaway." We must help our people to find these rock-hard principles, these unchanging values. It is what social researcher and well-known Keynote Speaker, Hugh Mackay, calls the task of preparing the rising generation of young people to find 'the inner resources for coping with discontinuity'. We want them to be people who can live their lives at depth, a depth where superficial changes do not disturb them. It is training them to be truly free, to stand against unthinking slavery of any form—habits that change, changing opinions, idols of clay or congratulation.'

C Gleeson SJ, 'The Value of Values', Johnson & Johnson
Leadership Forum, Duntroon, September 1997

Ω

'Everyone who comes to me and listens to my words and acts on them—I will show you what such a person is like. Such a person is like the man who, when he built a house, dug, dug and dug deep, and laid the foundations on rock; when the river

was in flood it bore down on that house but could not shake it,
it was so well built.'

Luke 6:47–48

'One regret, dear world,
That I am determined not to have
When I am lying on my deathbed
Is that
I did not kiss you enough.'

The Persian Poet, Hafiz, quoted in Daniel J O'Leary, *Travelling
Light, op cit*, 190

Signpost—GOOD TEACHERS UTILISE THE POWER OF BLESSING WHEN THEY TEACH RIGHT VALUES —A SAMPLE STORY ABOUT LIGHTHOUSE VALUES

A

'This culture of relativism—where the prevailing belief is that anything is alright as long as it works for me—is the culture in which our young people live and breathe. This is the culture confronting missionaries in Christian Schools today. What can we do about it? In class and School Assemblies I have often returned to the naval story related by Stephen Covey in his excellent book, *The Seven Habits of Highly Effective People*:

> Two battleships assigned to the training squadron had been at sea on maneuvers in heavy weather for several days. I was serving on the lead battleship and was on watch on the bridge as night fell. The visibility was poor with patchy fog, so the captain remained on the bridge keeping an eye on all activities. Shortly after dark, the lookout on the wing of the bridge reported, 'Light, bearing on the starboard bow'. 'Is it steady or moving astern?' the captain called out. Lookout replied, 'Steady, captain,' which meant we were on a dangerous collision course with that ship. The captain then called to the signalman, 'Signal that ship: We are on a collision course, advise you change course 20 degrees.' Back came a signal, 'Advisable for you to change course 20 degrees.' The captain said, 'Send, I'm a captain, change course 20 degrees'. 'I'm a seaman second class,' came the reply. 'You had better change course 20 degrees.' By that time, the captain was furious. He spat out, 'Send, I'm a battleship. Change course 20 degrees.' Back

came the flashing light, 'I'm a lighthouse'. We changed course.

The meaning of this story is not lost on young people when it is explained that there are certain lighthouse values, lighthouse principles in our lives which are immutable and rock solid in lighting our path. Covey also refers to them as "true north principles"—values which have a truth of their own, independent of our particular standpoint or perspective. Professor Max Charlesworth once captured this beautifully in the following statement:

> Some things are *true* whether we think so or not; some things are *good* whether they suit our interests or not; some things are *just* whether or not they go counter to what we immediately want; some things are *beautiful* whether we happen to like them or not; some things are *sacred* whether we are willing to recognize them or not.'

C Gleeson SJ, 'The Sound of Eternity in the Midst of Change: Ministering to Young People in a Catholic School', in *Australian Catholic Record*, October 1998, LXXV, number 4: 395396

Ω

'There are a number of "lighthouse values", "true north principles", to which we must return again and again in schools. As teachers, administrators, and parents we are always looking for words that will be lighthouses—words which have a permanence about them, when everything else is change and fluid for our young people. In my Senior Religious Education Class, I have listed the following as "lighthouse statements" for a variety of topic areas:

- God is not just at the beginning and end of our journey, but in every step along the way.
- human life is sacred/precious at every point along the continuum from fertilization to death
- Rights and Responsibilities are co-relative; neither makes any sense without the other
- My rights are your responsibility
- the dignity of every human being is to be respected
- it is essential that I follow an informed conscience
- what is legal is not necessarily moral
- keep searching for the truth and when you find it, act on it, and it will set you free.
- with privilege goes responsibility.
- the quality of any community must be measured by the way it treats its weakest members.
- a strong community is a hospitable community.
- everyone has the right to be happy.'

Adapted from an article by C Gleeson SJ, 'The Sound of Eternity in the Midst of Change: Ministering to Young People in a Catholic School, *Australian Catholic Record*, as above

Signpost—GOOD TEACHERS UTILISE THE POWER OF BLESSING WHEN THEY TEACH RIGHT VALUES—A SAMPLE STORY ABOUT LIGHTHOUSE VALUES

A

'Tender moments are, of course, moments of grace—a sign of God's love at work in the world around us. Ronald Rolheiser reminds us in *Forgotten Among the Lilies* that "we need to pray by picking up the tender moment and letting its grace soften us. What constitutes the tender moment? Anything in life that helps make us aware of our deep connectedness with each other, of our common struggle, our common wound, our common sin, and our common need for help . . .".'

'Last week I was privileged to share another tender moment, a sacramental moment, at the final gathering of the Queensland Province of the Christian Brothers. As written elsewhere, the Brothers are repositioning themselves in the Church by becoming one Province of Oceania and dividing themselves into several geographical clusters within each State. The last session of the gathering was given to a blessing ceremony, when a Facilitator invited all the Brothers in age groups to come to the centre of the room for an individual blessing. As each specific age group was caught up in the Leader's rich words of blessing, the remaining Brothers came forward to place their hands on them in a beautiful gesture of "deep connectedness with each another". It recalled for me Paul's words in his second Letter to Timothy: "That is why I am reminding you now to fan into a flame the gift that God gave you when I laid my hands on you.".'

C Gleeson SJ, St Ignatius Parish Toowong newsletter,
July 15th, 2007

Ω

'Then Jesus said to the Twelve, "What about you, do you want to go away too?" Simon Peter answered, "Lord, to whom shall we go? You have the message of eternal life, and we believe; we have come to know that you are the Holy One of God.".'

John 6:67–68

Signpost—GOOD TEACHERS UTILISE THE POWER OF BLESSING WHEN THEY TEACH RIGHT VALUES —VALUES THAT ENDURE

A

'If the true leader, the proactive person, is value-driven in all that he or she does, what values are we talking about? Surely we mean those values which are lasting, have stood the test of time, and will not blow away with the first winds of change and fashion? If you were asked to enunciate a list of uncontroversial ethical truths, what would you come up with? One way to begin might be with the Ten Commandments and convert their largely negative prohibitions into positive statements to discover the positive values beneath them. We then establish the values of perspective, respect, celebration, family, choosing life, fidelity, stewardship, truth, and justice—strong and lasting values in anyone's language! The Archbishop of Canterbury, in a speech to the House of Lords, commented in these terms: "We take it for granted that you cannot play a game of football without rules. Rules do not get in the way of the game; they make the game possible. It is strange that what we take as so obvious for games, we deem unnecessary for life. That is not to trivialize what we are debating. Rules which make life worthwhile and keep relationships faithful and true are inextricably linked to the deepest things we believe about God and values which transcend us all. Our nation . . . has traditionally found our rules shaped by the Ten Commandments . . .".'

C Gleeson SJ, 'The Value of Values', *op cit*

Ω

'And now a lawyer stood up and, to test him, asked, "Master,
what must I do to inherit eternal life?" He said to him, "What
is written in the Law? What is your reading of it?" He replied,
"You must love the Lord your God with all your heart, with
all your soul, with all your strength, and with all your mind,
and your neighbor as yourself." Jesus said to him, "You have
answered right, do this and life is yours.".'

Luke 10:25–28

Signpost—GOOD TEACHERS UTILISE THE POWER OF BLESSING WHEN THEY REVEAL THE ENDURING VALUES WITHIN THE TEN COMMANDMENTS

A

Values and the Ten Commandments

Commandment	Value
'I am the Lord Your God . . .'	Perspective
'You shall not take the name . . .'	Respect
'Remember the Sabbath . . .'	Celebration
'Honor your father . . .'	Roots/Family
'You shall no kill . . .'	Choose Life
'You shall not . . . adultery'	Fidelity
'You shall not steal'	Stewardship
'You shall not . bear false witness . neighbour'	Truth
'You shall not cover . . . wife'	Justice
'You shall not covet . . . goods'	Justice

Ω

'Do not imagine that I have come to abolish the law or the Prophets. I have come not to abolish but to complete them.'

Matthew 5:17

Signpost—GOOD TEACHERS ARE BLESSING WHEN THEY ILLUSTRATE the ENDURING VALUES OF BEING AND GIVING

A

Values of Being and Values of Giving, Richard and Linda Eyre, *Teaching our Children Values* (New York: Simon and Shuster, 1993, 29)

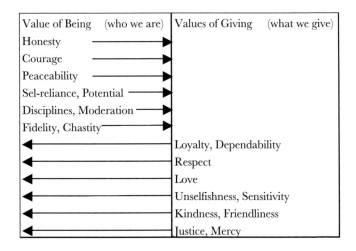

Value of Being (who we are)	Values of Giving (what we give)
Honesty	
Courage	
Peaceability	
Sel-reliance, Potential	
Disciplines, Moderation	
Fidelity, Chastity	
	Loyalty, Dependability
	Respect
	Love
	Unselfishness, Sensitivity
	Kindness, Friendliness
	Justice, Mercy

Ω

'Eternal life is not some great surprise that comes unannounced at the end of our existance in time; it is, rather, the full revelation of what we have been and have lived all along.'

Henri Nouwen, *Life of the Beloved* (New York: Crossroad, 1992), 109-110

Signpost—GOOD TEACHERS ARE BLESSING STUDENTS WHEN THEY TEACH VALUES THAT TRANSCEND CULTURAL DIFFERENCES

A

- which span all countries and cultures:
    - love
    - truthfulness
    - fairness
    - freedom
    - unity
    - tolerance
    - responsibility
    - respect for life

Ω

'There is a season for everything, a time for every occupation
under heaven:
A time for giving birth,
a time for dying;
a time for planting,
a time for uprooting what has been planted.
A time for healing;
a time for knocking down,
a time for building.
A time for tears,
a time for laughter;
a time for mourning,
a time for dancing.
A time for throwing stones away,
a time for gathering them;

a time for embracing.
A time for searching,
a time for losing;
a time for keeping,
a time for discarding;
A time for tearing,
A time for sewing;
a time for keeping silent,
A time for speaking.
A time for loving,
a time for hating;
a time for war,
a time for peace.'

Ecclesiastes 3:1–8

Signpost—GOOD TEACHERS UNDERSTAND THAT VALUES ARE CONTAINED IN THE EARLIEST LESSONS LEARNT AT KINDERGARETEN

A
'These Things I Learned at Kindergarten

❋ Share everything.

❋ Play fair.

❋ Don't hit people.

❋ Put things back where you found them.

❋ Clean up your own mess.

❋ Don't take things that aren't yours.

❋ Say you're sorry when you hurt somebody.

❋ Wash your hands before you eat.

❋ Flush.

❋ Warm cookies and cold milk are good for you.

❋ Live a balanced life—learn some and think some and draw and paint and sing and dance and play and work every day some.

❋ Take a nap every afternoon.

❋ When you go out into the world, watch out for traffic, hold hands, and stick together.

❋ Be aware of wonder. Remember the little seed in the Styrofoam cup: The roots go down and the plant goes up and nobody really knows how or why, but we are all like that.

❋ Goldfish and hamsters and white mice and even the little seed in the Styrofoam cup—they all die. So do we.

❋ And then remember the Dick-and-Jane books and the first word you learned—the biggest word of all—LOOK.'

From Robert Fulghum, *All I Really Needed to Know I Learned in Kindergarten* (London: Grafton Books, London, 1991), 6–7

Ω

'People were bringing little children to him, for him to touch them. The disciples scolded them, but when Jesus saw this he was indignant and said to them, "Let the little children come to me; do not stop them; for it is to these that the kingdom of God belongs. In truth I tell you, anyone who does not welcome the kingdom of God like a little child will never enter it." Then he embraced them, laid his hands on them and gave them his blessing.'

Mark 10:13–16

Signpost—GOOD TEACHERS UNDERSTAND THAT WE ARE BLESSED IN WAYS OFTEN UNIMAGINABLE

A

'We are often blessed in ways we can't imagine. Instead of getting what we want, we get what we need. The problem is that it takes longer to understand that what we didn't want is precisely what, in the end, was best for us.'

Joan Chittister OSB, *Listen With the Heart: Sacred Moments in Everyday Life* (Littlefield: Rowman & Littlefield, 2003), 8

Ω

The Bridge
'There are times in life when we are called to be bridges,
not a great monument spanning a distance
and carrying loads of heavy traffic, but a simple bridge to help
one person from here to there over some difficulty such as
pain, loneliness, grief or fear, a bridge which opens the way
for the ongoing journey.
When I become a bridge I bring upon myself a blessing,
for I escape from the small prison of self and exist for a far
wider
world, breaking out to be a larger being who can enter
another's
pain and rejoice in another's triumph.
I know of only one greater blessing in this life, and that is,
to allow someone else to be a bridge for me.'

Anonymous

Signpost—GOOD TEACHERS SHOW THAT THE ACT OF BLESSING LINKS US TO A LONG CHAIN OF PEOPLE AND EVENTS POINTING TO GOD

A

' . . . I usually recite a blessing, the *motzi*, before I eat. When I recite this ten-word, ancient formula, eating is transformed into an encounter with God. No longer is a muffin just a muffin, no longer is a sandwich two pieces of bread with something in between. Rather, eating becomes an encounter with God because the blessing reminds me that my food did not come from my refrigerator nor from my grocery store. Rather, it came to me via the rain, the sun, the people who tilled the soil and harvested the land and worked in the store which sold the food. When I recite the blessing, I become part of an awesome chain of people, events, and places which created my food. Once again, I can see the spark in all of these things, in all of these people.'

Rabbi Stacy Laveson in *How Can I find God?*, edited by James Martin (Missouri: Ligouri, 1997), 70

Ω

'I very much like the expression 'breaking bread together', because there the breaking and the giving are so clearly one. When we eat together we are vulnerable to one another. Around the table we can't wear weapons of any sort. Eating from the same bread and drinking from the same cup call us to live in unity and peace.'

Henri Nouwen, *Becoming the Beloved* (New York: Crossroad, 1992), 88

'He was seventy-five years old
and God's first word to him
was "go".

I think of Abram
when my plans go awry,
when happenstance

pries my fingers loose
from the grasping illusion
of control over life.

"Go" God said to Abram,
giving no address,
disclosing no destination.

Taking an unruly family,
trusting God to show the way,
Abram went.

On that wild journey
he, too, had fingers pried loose,
heard Sarai laugh, learned

the blessing comes
in the going
and the letting go.'

Bonnie Thurston, in Esther De Waal,
Lost in Wonder: Rediscovering the Spiritual Art of Attentiveness
(Melbourne: John Garratt, 2003), 93

Blessing myself is blessing the world

A

'I find making the sign of the cross over my mind, body and heart to be a deeply reconciling little ritual. As you touch your forehead and chest, in the Eastern tradition you are opening the brow and heart chakras of vision and compassionate understanding. According to Jewish practice, as you touch your left and right shoulder, you are activating the spiritual centres of mercy (*chesed*) and strength (*geburah*). In the Christian tradition we open ourselves to the influence of the Blessed Trinity, to the creator and sustainer of the world, to the saviour and reconciler of sins, to the healing spirit of new beginnings. In the end it is the Cross alone that will hold the opposites together and transform them. And only the light will then be transmitted. When I bless myself, the world too is blessed.'

Daniel J O'Leary, *The Tablet*

Ω

'Go, therefore, make disciples of all the nations; baptize them in the name of the Father and of the Son and of the Holy Spirit, and teach them to observe all the commands I gave you. And know that I am with you always; yes, to the end of time.'

Matthew 28:19–20

Teaching and Community-Building

When Jesus parted company with the two disciples after their meal together, they returned to their fearful community hiding from the Jews in a secret place. They said to one another: 'Did not our hearts burn within us as He talked to us on the road and explained the scriptures to us?' Jesus the consummate teacher had given them a new fire in the belly, a new understanding of their story, which they could then share with their friends to strengthen them and renew their resolve. All good teaching is about community-building, about life enlarging.

Signpost—GOOD TEACHING IS LIFE ENLARGING BECAUSE IT STRETCHES and STRENGTHENS THE HEART

A

'They set out that instant and returned to Jerusalem. There they found the Eleven assembled together with their companions, who said to them, "The Lord has indeed risen and appeared to Simon". Then they told their story of what had happened on the road and how they had recognized him at the breaking of bread.'

Luke 24:33–35

Ω

'At the 1998 AHISA Pastoral Care Conference in Sydney, the opening session was given to groups of students to dramatise what they considered to be the key issues in education of the heart. The themes from their various drama presentations were very clear—the need for a sense of belonging, loneliness and alienation, the classroom culture. I remember noting down a very stark line voiced by one young actress: "I am alone in this classroom full of people." It was a cry for community.'

C Gleeson SJ, 'However Apart we are Together', *The Dorothy Knox Lecture*, 2002

Signpost—GOOD TEACHING ENABLES STUDENTS TO LOOK OUT FOR OTHERS

A

'"We live in the shelter of each other", the old Irish proverb says. What a splendid image! School Principals and their staff are constantly challenging their students to look out for each other in the school community. Caring for one another is what strong communities do. Indeed, the quality of any community can be measured by the care it provides for its weakest members. 'None of us is as strong as all of us' was at one time the clever catch cry of fast food giant McDonald's. What a difference it would make to our world if we could all adopt the African philosophy of happiness expressed in the adage: "I am because we are"!'

Christopher Gleeson SJ, *A Canopy of Stars: Some Reflections for the Journey* (Melbourne: David Lovell, 2003), 11

Ω

'As it is, God has put all the separate parts into the body as he chose. If they were all the same part, how could it be a body? As it is, the parts are many but the body is one. The eye cannot say to the hand, "I have no need of you," and nor can the head say to the feet, "I have no need of you." What is more, it is precisely the parts of the body that seem to be the weakest which are the indispensable ones.'

1 Corinthians 12:18–23

Signpost—GOOD TEACHING HAS AN EYE TO BUILDING COMMUNITY BY ESPOUSING IDEAS OF SHARING, NOT HOARDING

A

'And all who shared the faith owned everything in common;
they sold their goods and possessions and distributed the
proceeds among themselves according to what each needed.
Each day, with one heart, they regularly went to the Temple
but met in their houses for the breaking of bread; they shared
their food gladly and generously; they praised God and were
looked up to by everyone. Day by day the Lord added to their
community those destined to be saved.'

Acts 2:44–47

Ω

'After all, community is the place where we learn to value and
respect each other, even if we don't always get our own way
or have our needs met. Here we learn that life is about us, and
not just about me. Community is that place where we learn to
value and honor people with whom we might not always get
along. Community, above all, is the place where we respect and
celebrate our differences.

Young people first learn about community, of course, in
the shelter of their family. What they learn or fail to learn in
the home they bring with them to the wider community of the
school family. Not surprisingly, then, many of the reflections in
this chapter point to the crucial importance of strong interaction
and understanding between home and school.'

C Gleeson SJ, *A Canopy of Stars, op cit,* 12

Signpost—GOOD TEACHERS KNOW THAT A STRONG SENSE OF BELONGING TO A COMMUNITY AT SCHOOL CAN PROTECT YOUNG PEOPLE AT RISK

A

'Okay, what about "Thank God it's Monday"? What would it take for people to look forward to Mondays?

I want three things out of Monday. 1) *community* – group of people—where we belong, where we can enjoy relationships of friendship, where we share a common vision. 2) a place where we can make a *contribution*—where the skills, interests and competence that we have can contribute something to the larger world—where who we are has value that is needed. 3) a place where we can continue to *grow and learn*—where we are taken seriously and encouraged to grow—where we have opportunity to learn and develop—both our ability to contribute and our ability to live life fully.'

Walter Wright, 'Relational Leadership', De Pree Leadership Center, Pasadena, California

Ω

'In the middle of the last century we saw our planet Earth from space for the first time. One of the first to see earth from space later wrote: "When you look at the earth from space . . . there are no national boundaries visible . . . It's a planet—all one place. All the beings on it are mutually dependent, like living on a lifeboat. Whatever the causes that divide us, the earth will be here a thousand—a million—years from now.

Michael Jordan, the great basketball player, said once: "There are plenty of teams in every sport that have great players and never win titles. Most of the time, those players aren't willing to sacrifice for the greater good of the team. The funny thing is, in the end, their unwillingness to sacrifice only makes individual goals more difficult to achieve . . . I'd rather have five guys with less talent who are willing to come together as a team than five guys who consider themselves stars and aren't willing to sacrifice. *Talent wins games, but teamwork and intelligence win championships."*

TS Eliot wrote: "What life have you if you have not life together? There is no life that is not in community, and no community not lived in praise to God." (*Choruses from 'The Rock')*

C Gleeson SJ, *A Canopy of Stars, op cit,* 18

Signpost—GOOD TEACHERS KNOW THAT BUILDING ONE STRONG PERSON IS BUILDING A STRONG BODY OF CHRIST

A

'In the same way, all of us, though there are so many of us, make up one body in Christ, and as different parts we are all joined to one another.'

Romans 12:5

Ω

'The words "Body of Christ" hold special meaning for me. About twenty years ago I started going to 9.05 am Mass after I dropped five of my six children to school. My three-year-old daughter, Jacinta, attended Mass with me, though she was not always too pleased to do so.

While waiting for the Mass to finish, she would sing out in a loud voice, 'Mum, when is the body of Christ?' When she heard the priest saying 'The body of Christ' while distributing communion it was the signal for her that Mass was almost over and we could soon leave.

We used to just nod and say hello to the regular Mass goers, not really getting to know anybody. However, after a few days of my daughter singing out 'Mum, when is the body of Christ?' three older parishioners who sat in a nearby pew asked me what she meant.

I explained to them about her impatience for the Mass to finish. That started a wonderful friendship. Frequently I would have a coffee in the local shopping centre with these three senior parishioners and they would buy Jacinta an ice-cream. More reason for Jacinta to ask, 'When is the body of Christ?'

Over the years our friendship grew. These three parishioners knew all the comings and goings in my life—my husband, children, work, and so on. Their faith and prayer life always amazed me.

I have had much illness, more operations than I can count. Each time I had an operation it would always be very important for them to know what time the surgery started and when it would finish. They would pray the expected length of the surgery.

Then as my children grew up and came to do their HSC, these three elderly parishioners would phone the day before each exam and ask "What time is the exam?" I would reply, "Between 9 and 12", "Between 2 and 4", or whatever. They would sit and pray for two or three hours during that exam. Needless to say, six children by six subjects by three hours amounted to a lot of praying time.

My three friends are now very elderly, one in a nursing home. As a minister of holy communion it is my great joy and privilege to bring them the Lord in the Eucharist.

"The body of Christ"—beautiful words for a beautiful friendship.'

Teresa Pirola's story on 'The Body of Christ', from *Madonna*
November–December, 2005

Signpost—GOOD TEACHERS HELP TO HOLD THE BALANCE BETWEEN US AND GOD

A

'Better two than one alone, since thus their work is really rewarding. If one should fall, the other helps him up; but what of the person with no one to help him up when he falls?'

Ecclesiastes 4:9–12

Ω

Assure Us that the Balance Holds

'The Irish poet Seamus Heaney has a poem *Weighing In* in which he says:

Passive

Suffering makes the world go round.

Peace on earth, men of good will, all that

Holds good only as long as the balance holds.

Post September 11, much of our public discourse even in Australia speaks of terror and fear. Many of our teenagers come from very conflicted families. It is almost as if their world is in free fall. In pastoral situations we have all known people whose lives are in such an emotional whirl that they hardly know which way is up. They are flat out looking after themselves, let alone worrying about anyone else. But as church we constitute a community—a community in which there will always be some members who are in free fall, a community which will always be immersed in a world of conflict and division. The gift of being a member of a human community boasting a variety of gifts in the one Spirit is the company of members whose lives and example assure us, when we are ready to hear and see with the eyes of faith, that no matter what the turmoil of the time, the balance holds between us and God. In the traumatic moments of modern youth, our students seek the assurance that the balance holds.'

An excerpt from Professor Frank Brennan's Address to the Sandhurst Catholic Secondary Education Conference—August 2004

Signpost—GOOD TEACHERS ARE KEEPERS OF THE COALS

A

'The Irish have the custom of burying warm coals in the ashes at night in order to preserve the fire for the cold morning to come. Instead of cleaning out the cold hearth, people preserved yesterday's glowing coals under beds of ash overnight in order to have a fast-starting fire the next day. Those of us in school, working with the parents at home, are the keepers of the coals. It is up to our graduates to ensure that they fan those coals into a fire of great warmth and light in their world of the future.'

C Gleeson SJ, *A Canopy of Stars, op cit*, 90

Ω

'That is why I am reminding you now to fan into a flame the gift of God that you possess through the laying on of my hands. God did not give us a spirit of timidity, but the Spirit of power and love and self-control. So you are never to be ashamed of witnessing to our Lord, or ashamed of me for being his prisoner; but share in my hardships for the sake of the gospel, relying on the power of God . . .'

2 Timothy 1:6–8

Signpost—GOOD TEACHERS LEAVE A POWERFUL LEGACY FOR GOOD

A

The Legacy of Leadership
- 'What are your children learning from you?
  - What makes you proud?
  - What makes you weep?
  - What would make you resign?
  - What legacy are you leaving now?'

Walter Wright, 'Relational Leadership' *op cit*

Ω

'"You are a member of the British royal family", Queen Mary said to her daughter Queen Elizabeth. "We are never tired and we all love hospitals." There are things we do in life because the groups to which we belong require that they be done by us or they may not be done at all.'

Joan Chittister OSB, *Listen with the Heart: Sacred Moments in Everyday Life, op cit*, 65

'For I shall take you from among the nations and gather you back from all the countries, and bring you home to your own country. I shall pour clean water over you and you will be cleansed; I shall cleanse you of all your filth and of all your foul idols. I shall give you a new heart, and put a new spirit in you; I shall remove the heart of stone from your bodies and give you a heart of flesh instead. I shall put my spirit in you, and make you keep my laws, and respect and practice my judgments.'

Jeremiah 36:24–27

Signpost—GOOD TEACHERS BUILD STRONG COMMUNITIES

A

'I, the prisoner in the Lord, urge you therefore to lead a life worthy of the vocation to which you were called. With all humility and gentleness, and with patience, support each other in love. Take every care to preserve the unity of the spirit by the peace that binds you together. There is one Body, one spirit, just as one hope is the goal of your calling by God. There is one Lord, one faith, one baptism, and one God and Father of all, over all, through all and within all.'

Ephesians 4:1–6

Ω

(The following address by Walter Wright, a visiting lecturer in Sydney at the time, I found very helpful on the topic of building community in the work place. In writing to thank him for these ideas, I said that they had excellent application in schools. CG)

Personal Values in Community People

1. **People have intrinsic worth**: Peter Drucker and Max De Pree consider this the fundamental value of human organizations—*the foundation of relationships*—and I would add: the key to community.
2. **Everyone should make a commitment to the mission**: the organization makes space for individual members to make a meaningful commitment to

the mission which binds this particular community together

3. **People who work with us should grow.** Participating in the . . . community should result in growth professionally, personally and spiritually. The whole person should develop because of participation in our company. Back to the balance between Monday and Friday.

4. **No one should take themselves too seriously.** A proper perspective in the organization puts the needs of others ahead of our own.

5. **All people should be seen as contributing peers, regardless of their scope of responsibility.** Contributing members of the community stand as peers and partners in pursuit of the mission even though different levels of responsibility may be defined by the organizational structure.

6. **Leadership should be empowering.** Leaders are present in the community to ensure the success of the other members of the organization. The question is not: 'who reports to you?' But: 'for whose success are you responsible.'?

Work

7. **Mission of the organization normally takes precedent over individual purposes.** The shared purpose that brings the organization into existence should be placed ahead of the agenda and purposes of individual members of the community—even though we hope people will be able to achieve some of their personal agendas through our corporate mission.

8. **Participation produces ownership of results.** The involvement of people in the development of organizational plans and strategies should result in stewardship of the mission and ownership of the intended results.

9. **The workplace should provide community.** As a place where people spend the majority of their life, the workplace should facilitate the development of supportive, caring friendships. Thank God it's Monday!

10. **People should have fun and find joy in their work.** A healthy organization will give people satisfaction and joy in return for the investment of their efforts and encourage an environment in which we can laugh with one another. Oxford Professor, Theodore Zeldin, told *Fast Company* recently that companies will find profitability when they reinvent work to allow people to do work that they find enjoyable. (*LA Times,* January 7, 2001.)

11. **We should always provide professional service in a friendly environment.** Professional quality and caring community are necessarily complementary.

Relationships

12. **Truth is found in dialogue.** Truth is more apt to be found in a community in dialogue than in an individual in isolation.

13. **Information is friendly.** A healthy organization communicates openly, shares information and promises no surprises to its members. I am currently working with an organization that is plagued by a culture of secrecy. Everyone feels excluded.

14. **Confrontation is a sign of caring.** People who care for people hold them accountable to their values and growth. Confrontation is holding you accountable to *your* values because I care about *you*.

15. **Criticism without constructive action is destructive gossip.** Confrontation or criticism without caring and positive action is destructive to the individual and the organization. Criticism is holding you accountable to *my* values because I care about *me*.

16. **Honesty, integrity and trust are essential in everything we do.** Everything I have said above rests on a foundation of trusting relationships. Without trust the organization and the community will die. A new book out of the Harvard Business School, *In Good Company*, (written by James Martin SJ) argues that trust is the social capital that builds the networks absolutely required for survival in a fast changing world.

17. **Forgiveness should characterize our life together.** Everyone makes mistakes. An organization with a 'second-chance character' learns from mistakes.

From Walter Wright, 'Relational Leadership', De Pree Leadership Center, California: a paper delivered in Sydney

Signpost—GOOD TEACHERS POSSESS A COMMUNITY-BUILDING TRANSPARENCY ABOUT THEM

A

'An argument started between them about which of them was the greatest. Jesus knew what thoughts were going through their minds, and he took a little child whom he set by his side and then he said to them, 'Anyone who welcomes this little child in my name welcomes me; and anyone who welcomes me, welcomes the one who sent me. The least among you all is the one who is the greatest.'

Luke 9:46–48

Ω

'When I'm in the control tower, my head provides all the answers—they're clear-cut, absolute, allowing of no conversation or adjustment. They never listen to the cry of my heart, the profound need I have for growth, for mystery, for love, for adventure, for intimacy. My head-answers save me from all of these—I wear a tie to keep my heart quite separate from my head (Leunig) – nothing flows between the two—it's too risky.'

Kevin Bates SM, 'Walking on Water: an improbable invitation?!' From his website www.kevinbates.com

Signpost—GOOD TEACHERS UNDERSTAND THAT ANYTHING CAN BE BORNE IF IT CAN BE SHARED

A

'There is a loneliness that can be spoken of because its pain is greater than its shame. It drives you to your knees, but also more deeply into humanity.

Nature equips you to deal with this. This kind of loneliness hurts you but it does not change you. It can be talked about, no small thing: *Anything can be borne if it can be shared.*

But there is a loneliness that cannot be shared, which is "unspeakable" because it is experienced in a way so private and humiliating that, were you to speak of it, you would further damage an already over-fragile sense of self that has been made so fragile by the loneliness itself.'

Ronald Rolheiser, 'Share your unspeakable loneliness', in *The Western Catholic Reporter*, week beginning 15 November 2004

Ω

'A few years ago I was told of one of the terrible moments in Bosnia. It concerned a number of Catholic religious sisters who were raped by the Serb militia. One of them, Sister Lucy, wrote a letter to her superior expressing her torment and also the painful decision to leave religious life in order to give herself fully to being a mother of the child she was now expecting as a result of the rape. She had taken vows only a year before the night when these soldiers repeatedly abused her for hours. In her letter to her superior she recalled how she had pious thoughts of offering herself as a martyr "but not like this!" Her letter described not so much the horrible event itself but rather the aftermath, her total sense of shock at finding her imagined life destroyed. "My trauma is not just the humiliation I suffered as a woman, nor the unhealable wound to my religious consecration, but the difficulty with squaring what happened with my faith, of seeing it as somehow part of the mysterious will of the One I considered as my divine spouse." Her letter ended "I will go with my child, I don't know where, but God, who so suddenly broke my joy, will show me the road. My child, born from violence, will learn only love. Together we will witness the greatest thing a human being can do is to forget.".'

Quoted in a speech by Peter Hosking SJ, '"Ignatius"' Vision about a Mission of Faith and Justice', Xavier College, 27 January 1999

Signpost—GOOD TEACHERS UNDERSTAND THAT THEIR COMMUNITY-BUILDING WORK IS AN EXERCISE IN FAITH

A

The Teacher as Sower—teachers are spring-time workers, planting the seeds of right judgment and discernment for the future, often not seeing short-term rewards for their work but knowing that they are contributing something to the wider community for the long term. Teaching is an act of faith. Cardinal Hume once called teaching 'iceberg work', because so much of what we achieve goes on beneath the surface in the minds and hearts of our young people. Sir Richard Livingstone, at one time President of Corpus Christi College Oxford, said that there 'is in education a law of delayed action, by which seeds sown and long forgotten only grow in later years. Teachers like to see results from their efforts, and direct them accordingly. But the most precious fruits of a good teacher's work are those that he is never likely to see.'

In this context, the words of Oscar Romero, Archbishop of San Salvador in 1980, are also very appropriate for our work in schools:

'It helps now and then to step back and take the long view.
The kingdom is not only beyond our efforts,
it is even beyond our vision.
We accomplish in our lifetime only a tiny fraction
of the magnificent enterprise that is God's work.
Nothing we do is complete, which is another way of saying
that the kingdom always lies beyond us.

No statement says all that could be said.
No prayer fully expresses our faith.
No confession brings perfection,
no pastoral visit brings wholeness.
No program accomplishes the Church's mission.
No set of goals and objectives includes everything.
This is what we are about.
We plant the seeds that one day will grow.
We water seeds already planted,
Knowing that they hold future promise.
We lay foundations that will need further development.
We provide yeast that produces effects
Far beyond our capabilities.
We cannot do everything and there is a sense of liberation in
realizing that.
This enables us to do something, and to do it very well.
It may be incomplete, but it is a beginning, A step along the
way,
an opportunity for the Lord's grace to enter
and do the rest.
We may never see the end results,
But that is the difference
between the master builder and the worker.
We are workers, not master builders
ministers, not Messiahs.
We are prophets of a future not our own.'

Ω

'Again he began to teach by the lakeside, but such a huge crowd gathered around him that he got into a boat on the lake and sat there. The people were all along the shore, at the water's edge. He taught them many things in parables, and in the course of his teaching he said to them, "Listen! Imagine a sower going out to sow . . . Listen, anyone who has ears to hear!".'

Mark 4:1–3, 9

'My brother Joseph had Down's syndrome. Every so often, in my dreams, he still comes storming back to deeply disturb my life. My mother adored him. And during those most difficult times, especially when Joseph's severe diabetes demanded unrelenting attention, she was sustained by the certainty that in caring for Joseph she was entertaining angels unaware. If I had my mother back now I would tell her that it was even more than that. It was the Lord himself who was there.'

Daniel O'Leary, 'House's a Holy Place', *The Tablet*, 20 May 2006, 11

Signpost—GOOD TEACHERS UNDERSTAND THAT THEIR AUTHORITY HAS NOTHING TO DO WITH POWER AND EVERYTHING TO DO WITH COMMUNITY-BUILDING

A

'Just as what brings heat makes things expand
so it is the gift of love
to stretch hearts wide open; it is a warm and
glowing virtue.'

St John Chrysostom

Ω

'I want to beg you as much as I can . . . to be patient towards all that is unsolved in your heart and to try to love the questions themselves . . . Do not now seek answers which cannot be given you because you would not be able to live them. And the point is to live everything. Live the questions now. Perhaps you will then, gradually, without noticing it, live along some distant day into answer.'

Rainer Maria Rilke, *Letters to a Young Poet* (New York: Norton, 1954), 34–35

Signpost—GOOD TEACHERS UNDERSTAND THAT THEIR WITNESS IS A POWER FOR GOOD IN COMMUNITY-BUILDING

A

'Most of us go into teaching not for fame or fortune but because of a passion to connect. We feel deep kinship with some subject; we want to bring students into that relationship, to link them with the knowledge that is so life-giving to us; we want to work in community with colleagues who share our values and our vocation.'

Maryanne Confoy RSC, 'The Other Face of Spirituality: Faith Journeying in the New Millennium'

Ω

'Then Jesus spoke, "What do you want me to do for you?" "Rabbuni", the blind man said to him "Master let me see again." Jesus said to him, "Go, your faith has saved you". And immediately his sight returned and he followed him along the road.'

Mark 10:51–52

Signpost—GOOD TEACHERS ARE KEEPERS OF THE FIRE-THE SCHOOL'S VISION AND VALUES

A

'For the reality of school I turn to another culture, that of Kenya. I have been fortunate to visit Kenya twice. Kenyan culture is rich with tribal symbols and one in particular spoke powerfully to me about school and schooling. In Kenyan tribal culture, in the compound of the extended family, it is always one person's duty to be the keeper of the fire, so that the fire will never go out and the food is always kept hot ready for serving. For me the fire represents the vision and values which must be kept constantly alight in the hearts of both students and parents . . . The fire can go out if pupils lose their belief in themselves. Just as a crowd always gathers around a good fire, when the vision and values of a school are clearly named, often articulated and made concrete in the day to day life of the school, students, parents and the local community will gather. Research has shown that such a school will be a vibrant community, with committed students, teachers and parents, which will achieve good academic results together with excellent personal and social development.'

Sr Pat Murray IBVM, 'Daring to be an educator', a talk given at the Loreto Schools' Network Day, 22 November 1997

Ω

'Where there is no vision the people perish.'

Proverbs 29:18

Signpost—GOOD TEACHERS HELP THEIR STUDENTS TO BECOME PILGRIMS IN THE WORLD, NOT TOURISTS

A

'In reflecting on the Gospel story of the two disciples journeying to Emmaus after the Resurrection of Jesus, we can see the metaphor of the Pilgrim as a very helpful pathway to gaining in virtue, strengthening our character. Somewhere in his prodigious writings, Chief Rabbi of the Commonwealth, Jonathan Sacks, distinguishes between the pilgrim and the tourist. Pilgrims are those people who want to engage with the world and not be mere spectators, people whose goal is less to reach a particular destination than to be transformed in the journey itself. A tourist goes somewhere to see something new, while a pilgrim goes somewhere to *become* someone new. Indeed, tourism protects tourists from becoming someone new by insulating them from the unfamiliar or the uncomfortable.'

C Gleeson SJ, Homily at AHISA (Association of Heads of Independent Schools of Australia) Pastoral Care Conference, 2006

Ω

'The City which forgets how to care for the stranger has forgotten how to care for itself.'

Homer, *The Odyssey*

Signpost—GOOD TEACHERS SEE THEIR ROLE AS MISSIONARIES

A

'Those of us working in Christian schools often see ourselves as missionaries, as people who endeavour to bring the Gospel to young people and others where they are, not where we would like them to be. Vincent Donovan writes beautifully of the missionary role:

> When the gospel reaches a people where they are, their response to that gospel is the church in a new place, and the song they will sing is that new, unsung song, that unwritten melody that haunts all of us. What we have to be involved in is not the revival of the church or the reform of the church. It has to be nothing less than what Paul and the Fathers of the Council of Jerusalem were involved in for their time—the refounding of the Catholic church for our age."[1]

Where precisely is this "new place" inhabited by the youth in our schools? Perhaps it is best described as a maelstrom of change, where nothing is permanent and change is the only constant. Social researchers like Hugh Mackay have demonstrated to us very clearly that the unprecedented rate of change in Australia in the past three decades has produced great anxiety, if not exhaustion, in the wider community. Hardly a convention or institution of Australian life has been left unchallenged or escaped our scepticism, if not cynicism. Social commentators have various ways of describing this—for example, as a "crisis of values", "morality at the crossroads", or as a "hole in the

---

1. Vincent J Donovan, *Christianity Rediscovered* (New York: Orbis, 1989), vii.

moral ozone layer". Clearly, a loss of morality has led—and
this is no mere word play—to a loss of morale. Writing in *The
Australian Magazine*, journalist Kate Legge observed starkly:
"Sometimes it seems as if society's moral voice has been buried
in an avalanche of information. We have junked the taboos
which sought to preserve allegiance to institutions such as
Church and family and framed an alternative code of conduct
which is more concerned with etiquette than ethics. We are too
fragmented and confused to agree on a common core of values.
Decriminalisation, deregulation, and the roar of capitalism have
freed us to live or die as we choose".'[2]

C Gleeson SJ, "'The Sound of Eternity in the Midst of
Change": Ministering to Young People in a Catholic School',
in the *Australian Catholic Record, op cit*

Ω

'We live in a new world, which Zygmunt Bauman of Leeds and
Warsaw Universities calls "Liquid Modernity". In this world,
what circulates are . . . images, logos, symbols, and signs. We live
in what has been called "the symbol saturated society".'

Timothy Radcliffe OP, *What is the Point of Being Christian?*
(London: Burns and Oates, 2006), 18

---

2. Kate Legge, *The Australian Magazine*, June 22/23, 1996

Signpost—GOOD TEACHING RENEWS THE WORLD

A

One could not find a better statement of the nobility of our teaching ministry to young people than the words of an early Jesuit school master—*'institutio puerilis renovatio mundi'*—'the education of youth is the renewal of the world'.

Ω

'Everyone is a house with four rooms:
A physical, a mental, an emotional and a spiritual.
Most of us tend to live in one room most of the time.
But unless we go into every room, every day
Even if only to keep it aired, we are not a complete person.'

Proverb from India

Signpost—GOOD TEACHING RENEWS THE WORLD

A

'In his excellent book, *Morality and the Adolescent*, psychologist Charles Shelton argues that adults ministering to young people must help them "frame" their decisions and choices. He uses the word "frame" deliberately, because he believes it is the adult's task to provide images or pictures to assist the young person in the decision-making process. Just as pictures have frames to heighten imaginative immediacy and intensify emotional identification, so too we as teachers and administrators must help young people "frame" the pictures that fire their imaginations. After all, the imagination provides the adolescent with another way of seeing himself or herself and their world. It is a route to their hearts, their deeper selves.'

C Gleeson SJ, 'Quality of Soul: Spirituality in Schools', *Dialogue* article as above

Ω

'In our world today riddled by division and fear, the basic tenets of hospitality need to be revisited and embraced by all of us. It lies at the heart of religion as connectedness. To be a true host, we must be open to the dignity of each and every person, ever prepared to leave behind our baggage of false assumptions and resentments, ready to receive the stranger on his or her own terms. As Henri Nouwen has described it so well, hospitality can be offered only by those who "have found the centre of their lives in their own hearts".'

Not surprisingly, Kathleen Norris comes to the conclusion that hospitality is at the center of our Christian faith. Monastic hospitality is a shining example for all of us. "In a world in which we are so easily labeled and polarized by our differences: man/woman, Protestant/Catholic, gay/straight, feminist/ chauvinist, monastic hospitality is a model of the kind of openness that we need if we are going to see and hear each other at all". (*The Cloister Walk*, 162) For the Christian this theme is highlighted in the Eucharist where the bread of life is our "host".'

C Gleeson SJ, 'Giving Religion a Good Name', in AHISA (Association Heads of Independent Schools of Australia) magazine *Independence*, no 2, 2003.

Signpost—GOOD TEACHING UNDERSTANDS THAT HOSPITALITY IS OPENNESS TO CHANGE

A

'What a difference it would make if I were to welcome everything that happens as good news. It may require some extra digging in some situations to get beneath the surface affront to discover the pleasant surprise, but what a different person I would be if I were to jettison my readiness to qualify everything unexpected as bad news.'

Michael Casey, *Fully Human Fully Divine: An Interactive Christology* (Melbourne: John Garrat, 2004), 151

Ω

In the words of an old Irish wish:

'May the raindrops fall lightly
On your brow
May the soft winds freshen your spirit
May the sunshine brighten your heart
May the burdens of the day rest lightly
Upon you
And may God enfold you in the mantle
Of his love.'

Signpost—GOOD TEACHING UNDERSTANDS THE POST-MODERN CONTEXT IN WHICH OUR STUDENTS LIVE

A

'While some theologians refer to it as "the dreaded P word", postmodernism is the cultural context in which our young people live and, as such, is the only context within which we may address them. At the recent Dialogue Australasia conference in April this year, British educator Jeremy Hall summed up Postmodernism as follows:

> Postmodernism moves beyond the 'modern' scientifically based view of the world by blending scepticism about technology, objectivity, absolutes and total explanations with a stress on image and appearance, personal interpretation, pleasure and the exploration of every spiritual and material perspective.

On the positive side of the ledger, postmodernism has seen a return to religion and spirituality. While this has not translated into increasing numbers going to mainstream churches, people are once again asking religious questions. The purely rational and the secular no longer seem to satisfy. For young people, postmodern times have allowed them to revel in greater choice and personal discovery. Just as the Internet has become the symbol of postmodern culture, so the supermarket is its supreme metaphor and the shopping mall its cathedral. Postmodernity is open to all possibilities. Everything is on display and on offer.

On the down side, there are many negative aspects of postmodernism. "There is no big picture of life or ultimate meaning in the universe. We are an instant generation looking for what works. We are highly doubtful about whether there are any absolute truths except what we come up with ourselves. We want to have fun. We want the good things in life and we want them here and now. Our needs are at the centre of our existence. Appearance is reality; so what matters is style and image . . . the ultimate evil is being bored".'

C Gleeson SJ, *Dorothy Knox Lecture*, 2002

Ω

'Hospitality is the ability to make another person comfortable in strange space: ours.'

Joan Chittister OSB, *Light in the Darkness: New Reflection on the Psalms for Every Day of the Year* (New York: Crossroad, 1998), 94

Signpost—GOOD TEACHING UNDERSTANDS THAT HOSPITALITY IS OPENNESS TO CHANGE

A

'Melbourne pediatric physician Dr John Court posits that young people inhabit four worlds—their family, their school (work), their social world, and their inner world. Each world has its own language which is often indecipherable to those outside their world, and intentionally so. Not only must they live in different worlds, but the young seek to find belonging in these worlds too. If a youth does not feel at home in one world, he or she may gain strength from another. The greater the separation of the youth's four worlds, and the less they overlap, the greater the risk to the child, because it lessens the opportunity for one world to provide strength to another.

What, then, can we teachers offer in the way of spiritual connectedness for our young people? Let us focus here on their "inner world", understanding that good teachers of their very nature do a great deal every day to build a strong *school* world for their students. Perhaps some of the astonishing success of John Marsden first as a teacher and now as a writer for teenagers, is his ability to help them explore and understand their inner world—their spiritual self.'

C Gleeson SJ, *Dorothy Knox Lecture*, 2002

Ω

In the Scriptures hospitality to the stranger is connected to the presence of God. 'Whoever welcomes you, welcomes Me.'

'Hospitality to the stranger is a shortcut formula expressing the core of the Christian vision.'

Lucien Richard, *Living the Hospitality of God* (Denville, NJ: Dimension Books, 2000), 78

A FINALE—NEVER STOP DANCING OR SINGING!

'After a bomb killed two dozen people at a Tel Aviv disco a few years ago, Israeli youth refused to be cowed. They resumed a robust nightlife. Today, outside the scene of the bombing, beneath a stone memorial listing the names of the dead, is a single inscription: Lo Nafseek Lirkod. It means "We won't stop dancing".'

Gene Weingarten, *The Washington Post Magazine*
Quoted in Gordon Livingstone, *And Never Stop Dancing: Thirty More True Things You Need to Know Now* (Sydney: Hodder, 2006)

Ω

SINGING MY SONG

'When a woman in a certain African tribe knows she is pregnant, she goes out into the wilderness with a few friends and together they pray and meditate until they hear the song of the child.

They recognise that every soul has its own vibration that expresses its uniqueness and purpose. When the women attune to the song, they sing it out loud. Then they return to the tribe and teach it to everyone else.

When the child is born, the community gathers and sings the child's song to him or her. Later, when the child enters education, the village gathers and chants the child's song. When the child passes through the initiation to adulthood, the people again come together and sing. At the time of marriage, the person hears his or her song. Finally, when the soul is about to pass from this world, the family and friends gather at the person's bed, just as they did at his birth, and they sing the person to the next life.

In the African tribe there is one other occasion upon which the villagers sing to the child. If at any time during his or her life, the person commits a crime or aberrant social act, the individual is called to the centre of the village and the people in the community form a circle around him. Then they sing his song to him. The tribe recognises that the correction for antisocial behaviour is not punishment; it is love and the remembrance of identity. When you recognise your own song, you have no desire or need to do anything that would hurt another.

There is something inside each of us that knows we have a song, and we wish those we love would recognise it and support us to sing it. How we all long to be loved, acknowledged and accepted for who we are!

A friend is someone who knows your song and sings it back to you when you have forgotten it. Those who love you are not fooled by mistakes you have made or dark images you hold about yourself. They remember your beauty when you feel ugly; your wholeness when you are broken; your innocence when you feel guilty; and your purpose when you are confused. If you do not give your song a voice, you will feel lost, alone and confused. If you express it, you will come to life.

We attract people on a similar wavelength so we can support each other to sing aloud. Sometimes we attract people who challenge us by telling us that we cannot or should not sing our song in public. Yet these people help us too, for they stimulate us to find ever greater courage to sing it.

We may not have grown up in an African tribe that sings our song to us at crucial life transitions, but life is always reminding us when we are in tune with ourselves and when we are not. When we feel good, what we are doing matches our song, and when we feel awful, it doesn't.

In the end, we shall all recognise our song and sing it well. We may feel a little warbly at times, but so have all the great singers. Just keep singing and you'll find your way home.'

Alan Cohen, '*They're Singing Your Song*', and an article from his web site

'Disturb us, Lord, when
We are too well pleased with ourselves,
When our dreams have come true
Because we have dreamed too little,
When we arrived safely
Because we sailed too close to the shore.

Disturb us, Lord, to dare more boldly,
To venture on wider seas
Where storms will show your mastery;
Where losing sight of land,
We shall find the stars.'

Sir Francis Drake the intrepid explorer

A Student to His Teacher
(published with permission)

'Dear Fr Chris,

I was delighted by your coming to the assistance of your old student recently, regarding my need for information about publishing.

I wonder if you remember the class of '77 in "RE" which you taught in that classroom opposite the tuck shop to we rather younger men back then? In forwarding a copy of this book, I would like to think you will find therein ample evidence that you had the ear of at least one of your students. In a time of quite some cynicism about faith and the worth of service, the effort of you and many of your colleagues made their mark and I assure you that there are plenty of us out here now who are doing their best to live up to now. Thanks again for your help.
With regards,
    Chris Howse.'

In 2007, Chris Howse published *Living Heart*, Charles Darwin University Press. It is an account of his work as a criminal lawyer on behalf of indigenous people in the Northern Tertory. His faith, courage, and perseverance in this work stem in part from the seeds sown by his teachers at Xavier College, Melbourne, thirty years on.

Epilogue: Teaching is Heart Work

'What we do with our hearts affects the whole universe.'
Congregation Chapter of Christian Brothers, Rome, 2002
'In a week of much travel I was in Sydney on Monday for a requiem Mass of Thanksgiving, which prevented me from attending a similar celebration in our own Parish on Tuesday afternoon. If ever I needed first hand confirmation of the Christian Brothers' statement, I experienced it in the palpable faith, honesty, and courage of the Joseph family and their friends last Monday at St Mary's Jesuit Church in North Sydney. Faced with the tragic loss of their only son and brother, Michael, they celebrated his life with such abundant love, hope, and humour that we, who were there to support them, were given life in the pain of it all. What the Josephs and Michael's beautiful young wife of just eight months did with their hearts that afternoon affected hundreds of people. We walked away from that Church taller, stronger, more loving and more grateful for the gift of life. With larger hearts we in turn will affect many others who, in God's providing way, chance to meet us on our journey.'

C Gleeson SJ, in St Ignatius Parish Toowong Newsletter,
2 July 2006

'It has been said that the longest journey we ever make is the journey to our heart. It is a journey that is never complete. And that is my message, my prayer, my hope for all of you graduates tonight—take good care of your hearts! Most of you will look after your bodies—give them adequate food and drink, exercise and watch your diets, and if you can afford one later in life when the body needs re-shaping, hire a personal trainer. But your heart needs caring for too.

I am not talking about that amazing little 11 ounce pumping unit in our chest that feeds a vascular system comprising 60,000 miles of veins and arteries and capillaries. If you are looking after your bodies, it is very likely that your heart pump will be in good working order too. No, I am talking about the heart which is your inner home, the centre of your being, the place which fuels your love, the place where you make the most important decisions, the place for finding the truth in your lives. The heart is you yourself, without any pretence, disguise, or make-believe. The heart is you.'

C Gleeson SJ, Address to the 2006 Graduation Class of St Patrick's College, Mackay, 13 November 2006

'A young substitute teacher sat beside me in the teachers' cafeteria. She was to start her regular teaching career in September and could I offer her any advice? Find what you love and do it. That's what it boils down to.'

Frank McCourt, *Teacher Man* (London: Fourth Estate, 2005), 255

'As good teachers weave the fabric that joins them with students and subjects, the heart is the loom on which the threads are tied, the tension is held, the shuttle flies, and the fabric is stretched tight. Small wonder, then, that teaching tugs at the heart, opens the heart, even breaks the heart—and the more one loves teaching, the more heartbreaking it can be . . .'

Parker Palmer, *The Courage to Teach*, folder of notes

'Sometimes life hits you in the head with a brick. Don't lose faith. I'm convinced that the only thing that kept me going was that I loved what I did. You've got to find what you love. And that is as true for your work as it is for your lovers. Your work is going to fill a large part of your life, and the only way to be truly satisfied is to do what you believe is great work. And the only way to do great work is to love what you do.'

Steve Jobs, CEO Apple Computer, commencement Address at Stanford University, 12 June 2005

'Your time is limited, so don't waste it living someone else's life. Don't be trapped by dogma—which is living with the results of other people's thinking. Don't let the noise of others' opinions drown out your own inner voice. And most important, have the courage to follow your heart and intuition. They somehow already know what you truly want to become.'

Steve Jobs, as above

'Desire is love trying to happen.'
Sebastian Moore, *Jesus the Liberator of Desire*

'For every mile the feet go, the heart goes nine.'
EE Cummings

'God is the heart and beyond of everything.'
Pierre Teilhard de Chardin SJ

'In a chapter entitled *Imo Pectore*—'in the innermost recesses of the heart'—Brian Doyle reflects on those Cardinals appointed by the Pope but, for political reasons, cannot be publicly announced. Their names are held by the Pope *imo pectore*. So it is with our own hearts. There are secret words in every heart. He reminds us that "our hearts are not pure: our hearts are filled with need and greed as much as with love and grace; and we wrestle with our hearts all the time. How we wrestle is who we are".'

C Gleeson SJ, 'All is Grace', in a review of Brian Doyle's *The Wet Engine: Exploring the Mad Wild Miracle of the Heart* in *Eureka Street*, January-February 2005

'Thus let me praise you in the way you love best, by shining on those around me. Let me preach without preaching, not by words but by example, by the loving influence of what I do, by the evident love my heart bears to you. Amen.'

Cardinal Newman

'One of the greatest privileges of being a teacher is to share in the discovery and excitement of each generation coming towards maturity. We all learn from the children in our care. As adults we never have all the answers. None of us is perfect. Often we struggle to find the right word or response to the unique child before us. As Sir Percy Nunn said in 1919, 'Teachers are ambassadors of society to the kingdom of the child".'

Bill Firman, *Sixty So Soon* (Melbourne: David Lovell Publishing, 2006), 95

'As teachers and parents, you kindle in your sons and daughters, a thirst for trust and wisdom. You spark off in them a desire for beauty. You introduce them to their cultural heritage. You help them to discover the treasures of other cultures and peoples. What an awesome responsibility and privilege is yours.'

Pope John Paul II

Index of Names

Biblical References